THE MODERN CONDITION OF EDUCATIONAL THOUGHT

THE MODERN CONDITION OF EDUCATIONAL THOUGHT

Bernd Pflug

GYAN PUBLISHING HOUSE

NEW DELHI - 110002

The Modern Condition of Educational Thought
(Education)

ISBN : 81-212-0688-X

Published in 2009 in India by
Gyan Publishing House
5, Ansari Road
New Delhi–110 002

Laser typesetting at: Sita Fine Arts Pvt. Ltd., Delhi–110 052

Printed by : Vishal Kaushik Printer

Dedicated to our daughters
Bharati and Rajeena

I won't teach a man who is not anxious to learn, and will not explain to one who is not trying to make things clear to himself. And if I explain one-fourth and the man doesn't go back and reflect and think out the implications in the remaining three-fourths for himself, I won't bother to teach him again.

Confucius

CONTENTS

PREFACE

The views expressed in this inquiry have been influenced by philosophers of education, both classical and modern, as well as by my own work as a teacher and educationist in various areas of the educational system. The experience gained there has not only confirmed the well-known fact that there is always a gap between educational theory and practice but also the truism that clear priorities help implement good education. These priorities will come about when practice is being reflected systematically and supported by arguments of purpose and, vice versa, when arguments of purpose are being scrutinized by practical experiments. This dialectical process also helps to clarify the two foundations on which education is built: the picture we have of human nature and the society, we consider to be a good one. Inquiries which can contribute to this dialectical process, I deem necessary in the philosophy of education.

This inquiry looks back, in particular, on more than a decade of teaching pupils between 14 and 19 years of age. This long time can, by no means, be accounted for as wholly successful; that is why this look-back will evoke mixed feelings towards ideals and dreams never realized and also towards successes never expected. In this book I have tried, as detachedly as possible, to *generalize* the experiences made. It is not a 'postmodern' depth-account but, I do hope, an analysis based upon the firm belief in the power of education as enlightenment and what I regard as one of the strongest impulses of modern philosophical reflection, "to salvage the claims of rational universalism while acknowledging the full force and import of contingency and history."[1]

This contribution to modern educational thought is not meant to produce a theory, say of curriculum-consciousness. It is not my ambition to build up a new theory which would have to satisfy logical consistency, empirical possibility, value conditions why it is so desirable, ideological neutrality, and judgmental relevance[2], nor it is my aim to simply rest on the "touchstone of experience" which has made, according to Jacob Needleman, modern philosophy so "easy"— "be it the experience of existentially crucial situations, the experience of perception, the experience of linguistic usage, the experience of moral decisions, the experience of emotions, or the experience of thinking and judging."[3]

What I have intended is much simpler than building a theory and yet, at least I assume, a sophisticated attempt to philosophize in the 'experience of linguistic usage' because this inquiry has something to do with language and failure. This failure is only to be understood through a reflection on the language I used for conceptualizations as a teacher. I did not realize for many years that the incongruence between thought and practice was subject to a wrong use of language in particular instances of my work. To put it succinctly, I mixed essentialist and contextualist usage of concepts and ended up, as probably so many in our profession, with an immense gulf between intention and action. I have used this inquiry to clarify this failure for myself and others, by addressing at the same time the ultimate Socratic challenge—on what right, on what authority, can anyone presume to teach?

But let me make it clear that though I have felt confident to reflect on some fundamentals in teaching and learning, this philosophizing must not, however, be mistaken for the imparting of wisdom acquired in the latter stage of a career. I am not blessed with such a wisdom at all because there are, for me, still too many uncertainties in the rather mundane work of education, not least of them philosophical. And since to wonder about the things of everyday knowledge is one of the deep sources of philosophizing, I have taken up some of these general problems which will probably continue to trouble us in education.

If in this inquiry I have sounded, at times, rather categorical, it is not necessarily the outcome of certainty but more so of a conviction that we have to stand in education for something that we dare have a standpoint. And when I have appeared rather harsh on attitudes, thoughts and behaviour of teachers in general, it is not to demean a whole profession which accounts for numerous exceptions, but to include myself into those I criticize. Over-generalizing has been used only to help focus on a problem.

Since this inquiry was never meant to be a therapeutic postmodern one which would have looked for the good feeling of a like-minded group, acknowledgments are not necessary. They read in today's academic world sometimes like catalogues of indebtedness and one wonders what really was the contribution of the author. Too often are they an indication of trying to clinch an argument by replacing 'speaking for oneself' with 'speaking for a like-minded community'. And judging from the lavish terms of gratitude and acknowledgment post-structural authors heap on their families and friends, students, editors, colleagues, and advisors—"generous, lovely, sagacious, hospitable, smart, funny, magnanimous, considerate, gracious, patient, caring, helpful, insightful, tactful, attentive, rigorous"—these authors already "inhabit the most idyllic intellectual community in the known world".[4] I am of the opinion that we should just work for a bit of the opposite: an unidyllic intellectual community in which everyone dares to know in his way[5], in which we try to be original and do not hide behind the convenient "anything goes".

Even Paul Feyerabend who has made this phrase and movement popular, looked back at it, shortly before his death in 1994, in a rather subdued manner:

> One of my motives for writing *Against Method* was to free people from the tyranny of philosophical obfuscators and abstract concepts such as 'truth', 'reality', or 'objectivity', which narrow people's vision and ways of being in the world. Formulating what I thought were my own attitude and convictions, I unfortunately ended up by introducing concepts of similar rigidity, such as 'democracy', 'tradition', or 'relative truth'. Now that I am aware of it, I wonder how it happened. The urge to explain one's own ideas, not simply, not in a story, but by means of a 'systematic account', is powerful indeed.[6]

And this is precisely the motivation for this inquiry too. Its statement can be summarized as follows:

> A condition of reflective educational thought is to develop modes of thought, that are both essentialist and contextualist. The former is in favour of a fixed canon of knowledge whereas the latter, while grappling with educational reality and factuality, is ready to replace old knowledge with new knowledge. Teachers and pupils together should practise these pedagogical modes of thought in a process I should like to call becoming conscious of

one's own curriculum. This process takes place in permanent operations of 'code-switching' between essentialist and contextualist concepts in communicative action.

This inquiry is being appended by two case studies for two reasons. First, to show that reflective educational thought is almost always a struggle between absolutistic ideas and their realization in different educational environments. This is also an underlying tread of the 'modern condition'. Second, the reader should have an opportunity to check the author's congruent—or not-so-congruent—thought in two practical cases in which the author has demonstrated how he thinks about his own role in an institution that follows a clear but impossible philosophy, and how he approaches the writing of a curriculum design. Though the confrontation of essentialism and contextualism is not mentioned in these case studies, the reader can assume that it was of vital importance for the author, not only while writing *about* the two practical examples but more so while being involved *in* them. The case studies are practical examples of pedagogical code-switching.

Bernd Pflug

References

1. J.M. Bernstein, 1995, p. 229.
2. See to this Gerald Dworkin, 1989, pp. 7-9.
3. See to this his argumentation in the essay "Why Philosophy is Easy?" pp. 12-22 in Jacob Needleman, 1994, p. 13.
4. From a book review by Elaine Showalter in *The Times Literary Supplement*, November 28, 1997, p. 28.
5. A note on the vexed he/she problem in thought and style. I think it should be solved by using the gender of the respective author instead by exercising stylistic acrobatics. Let female authors use throughout their works 'she', 'her', and so forth and let male authors do the same with 'he', 'him', and so forth. I am sure the meaning will trickle down to the readers.
6. Paul Feyerabend, 1995, pp. 179-180.

PART—I

THE MODERN CONDITION OF EDUCATIONAL THOUGHT

1

Epistemologies and Ordinary Educational Thought

Education is a human activity and, as such, subject to a number of conditions of which the interaction of thought and communication forms one important set. This set consists of activities about which epistemologies reflect—or not. Ordinary educational thought is dominated by these epistemologies.

The uncommon element in this thesis, perhaps, is the plural of epistemology. By epistemologies I mean not the one or other epistemology attached to a philosophical school which tries to espouse what knowledge is, what it is that can be known, and how it can be known; instead, by epistemologies I mean the manifestation of rather unorganized normative sets of beliefs which are thought right and good by teachers and are used by them as sources for their educational work. These sets of beliefs are considered by them (and by large sections of the public who send their children to schools where these teachers work) as *the* knowledge, i.e., the most important commodity in education and thus open to trade between and amongst the actors in education. This trade depends on the creation of a market for this knowledge and finds its biggest market in unorganized and organized education.

Teachers, barring exceptions, do not distinguish themselves much from the 'common' man with regard to knowledge production. Thus, I consider Santayana's seemly explanation of ordinary thought also applicable to teachers and their ways of forming knowledge:

> Custom does not breed understanding, but takes its place, teaching people to make their way contentedly through the world without knowing what the world is, nor what they think of it, nor what they are. When their attention is attracted to

some remarkable thing, say to the rainbow, this thing is not analysed nor examined from various points of view, but all the casual resources of the fancy are called for in conceiving it; and this total reaction of the mind precipitates a dogma; the rainbow is taken for an omen of fair weather, or for a trace left in the sky by the passage of some beautiful and elusive goddess. Such a dogma, far from being an interpenetration or identification of thought with the truth of the object, is a fresh and additional object in itself. The original passive perception remains unchanged; the thing remains unfathomed; and as its diffuse influence has by chance bred one dogma today, it may breed a different dogma tomorrow. We have, therefore, as we progress in our acquaintance with the world, an always greater confusion. Besides the original fantastic inadequacy of our perceptions, we have now rival clarifications of them, and a new uncertainty as to whether these dogmas are relevant to the original object, or are themselves really clear, or if so, which of them is true.[1]

These knowledge or sets of justified beliefs are acquired by teachers in their own process of socialization and are transmitted in educational practices to their pupils. Unclarified dogmas lead to further unclarified dogmas, and not many are really concerned. On the contrary, both teachers and pupils continue to love knowledge as dogmas even if they have been made aware of them. The reason for this is their familiarity with them. Parents would never want their son or daughter to learn that one plus one *could* equal three.

Now and then occasional updatings freshen these entrenched sets, but generally not beyond a cosmetic change by adding the latest fashion, and not doing much to overcome the "original fantastic inadequacy of our perceptions" and contributing, at best, to "rival clarifications". For example, a teacher of religion may add to his repertoire the latest results in physics only to have better arguments for the explanation of, say, monism he has always found the right way to explain the world. This teacher does not refer to physics to clarify a problem of cosmology for his pupils, nor does he do so to generate radical metaphysical doubt in his pupils which could lead to a dualistic understanding of life in which mind and matter are distinctive parts. (That nevertheless pupils may come to this and other conclusions is due to *their* robustness and motivation and not necessarily due to their teacher's intentions.)

Unorganized normative sets of justified beliefs, however, do oppose the scientific method of experimentation or controlled inquiry[2] which makes it possible for a body of knowledge to change and to grow, shedding all the time dogmas on its way. In G.H. Mead's words, when a problem has held us up, it is "the fact that we can carry on that guarantees our knowledge".[3] The irony of it is that a teacher may use a knowledge as dogma which was once created by a scientific method, but which he would now not put under further close scrutiny of experimental or controlled inquiry. Note that it can take generations to update textbooks . An illustration would be to follow up the latest and new results concerning the 'The Indus Valley Civilization' and whether and when they would reach eventually the textbook stage (not meaning, of course, the politically motivated inclusions of 'correct' history).

Unorganized normative sets of justified beliefs remain stationary since they are not exposed to doubts by those who have them; they are neither hypothesized nor tested by imaginative action and reasons. We have, therefore, to assume that another interest plays a key role in the selection and formation of knowledge in the ordinary educational thought of teachers.

Following Habermas's three-fold classification of human interests into technical cognitive interest (which plays a major role in empirical analytical sciences), practical interest (which determines historical-hermeneutic sciences), and emancipatory cognitive interest (which inspires so-called critically oriented sciences)[4], we have to ask where we would locate ordinary educational thought. It is all very well to locate a science of education, for example, in the third group, but what to do when ordinary educational thought is just all exercise of repetition of knowledge and a perpetuation of a social situation in which a teacher does not express such concern aroused by, for instance, intellectual curiosity or the possibility of societal change? We still have to call this functioning 'interest' since all dealing with knowledge is related to some human interests though not necessarily transcending human experience and imagination.[5]

Interest as a mover of ordinary educational thought takes over the rather pragmatic task of motivating a teacher to do something. That is why its prime function is to help in decision-making when it comes to decide what to teach how. This interest is determined by the personal interest of a teacher to perform in some way or the other or the socio-political interest of a society to survive unchanged (in which case ordinary educational thought is being complemented by ordinary social thought of a wider societal group). Interest is the main mover of ordinary epistemologies insofar as it is one of the dominant forces of human nature (the others being love and power).

Teachers build up over time their epistemologies which they think should help create particular perceptions in pupils. However, these epistemologies are characterized not so much by coherence and depth (if they were, we could confidently operate with the singular of epistemology) but by omni-comprehensiveness of content, assuming that *more* knowledge of the *same* kind is better education. Hence the accumulation of knowledge is promoted for the sake of a—misrepresented—value: to know. In this understanding, to know means to have or to do something good; in education, to know is hardly ever associated with something bad in particular; the activity to know is per se a good one and inherits a value which should be striven for. In the end it matters more *that* we know something and not *what* we know. Scores of teachers are caught in this trap.

Here we are now faced with the problem that teachers easily fall into the habit of not clarifying the meaning of knowledge they teach but take it for granted since it is part of a tradition or canon. They prefer not to ask the question what is the grammar for the use of this knowledge?[6] They do not question selection procedures either unless they are delegated into an official committee which has been established by an authority for this purpose. Instead, they prefer to operate with vague or increasingly utilitarian ideas about the nature and use of knowledge which do not do justice to an analysis of meaning of knowledge as an essentially cognitive judgment.

Once set in the iron frame of a syllabus, once having it made to the canon, the knowledge teachers have to teach becomes, for them, non-questionable and non-analyzable because if they did question and analyze, they would have to think critically about their own society and themselves. They would have to do so because knowledge could be understood as a product of a cooperative action[7], and "(n)othing that is knowable by one person alone can have the status of knowledge".[8] This action of non-clarifying leads then to the construction of hybrid epistemologies teachers tend to have, all of which have in common that they do not question the purpose of having and creating this or that knowledge and the purpose of transmission of this knowledge.

That is why we may argue that ordinary educational thought is dominated by an apathy of purpose. A first explanation for this apathy is that in ordinary educational thought the *process* of education is not permanently reflected. In any educational process a teacher is supposed to practise the art of satisfying the educational needs of as many pupils as possible in one group. This demands of him to take every individual pupil intellectually, socially and physically serious. Such a challenge cannot even be contemplated by the average teacher because of the large number of pupils he has to teach. Moreover, the argument that the syllabus is set and applies to all pupils in a like manner, makes a discussion of the needs of pupils redundant for most of them. Such a practice of whole-group teaching has been, over time, widely equated with 'education'.

But this is not the only reason which prevents teachers from reflecting on the educational process. A more important one is that this reflection is considered by many as superfluous. They argue that it is the pupil who has to adjust to a given educational environment by absorbing as much as he can from the content taught with techniques which have worked in the past. This is not only neglecting the individual development of a pupil, it is also depriving him of the human environment he needs in order to feel that the things taught are not mysteries. He also misses out on the possibility that the things taught do not belong to school only but are facts and ideas which belong to life outside school too.

Such an understanding of the role of a teacher is ultimately shifting the responsibility for reflection on the pupil who has then to make the best of this 'offer'. The 'offer' is, however, not an offer but a dictat, and the reflection is not a reflection but a command. The desired result is not the reflective pupil but a highly competitive one who designs clever ways of adaptation to be successful. The teacher feels justified to continue with his common programme in a common style because there are always some pupils who respond 'properly' to his offer. Those who respond so, do thus legitimize the teacher's style and approach and blame the rest of the class for their relative failure on not trying hard enough which, the silent majority it is, is being accepted by them without much ado. So both the protagonists, the teacher as well as the pupil, feel quite set in a system which occurs to them as rightfully standardized. In this approach, knowledge is being formed and imposed on pupils with a sense of urgency; it is being pursued breathlessly and assessed ruthlessly as though everybody's life is depended upon it.

The second explanation for the apathy of purpose is that teachers tend to underestimate the complex nature of knowledge and do limit it to a social role. The latter is, however, hardly evaluated in a critical mode which would examine why a societal system has created a particular type of knowledge and how it may create a new system of thought or perpetuate the old one. Instead, to limit knowledge uncritically to a social role, like getting the right for a particular employment, is to use knowledge to perpetuate a system which is not being questioned why it is as it is, what its purpose is, and whether it could or should be changed. This understanding of knowledge in education breeds its own epistemologies or justification. They appear today to be more eclectic than consistent, more calculating than discovering, more linear than chaotic, and more geared towards immediate applicability than to enjoyment.

To advance an argument which will occupy us later in greater detail: these epistemologies document in part a post-modern mood with its absence of historical criteria and not one of emancipation enthused by the enlightened understanding of the mutual dependency of individual and society. Questions whether knowledge can guarantee employment and social status take precedence over those which, for instance, elaborate on the kind of inferences which could be deduced from a in order to arrive at *b*, or which meaning could be explored in *c* through *d*. Facts and ideas are willed to be stationary, unambiguous, uncritical. Hence it is normal to overlook the steady tension which exists between subjectivity and inter-subjectivity and, instead, indulge in adjusting and obeying. Exercising in curriculum design may thus predictably end up as drab administrative procedures rather than as dramatic intellectual climaxes over what to make out of a potential '1+1=3' problem. If teachers (and with them planners) were exposed to such curricular tension and willing to take it as an entry point into the permanent reflection of educational process, their well-set epistemologies would be shaken up and finally produce something as meaningful as knowledge and knowledge transmission. Such a reflection of educational process might then be regarded as part of curriculum studies the concern of which is to conceptualize the practice of education and hence could assume "a form of applied philosophy".[9]

Epistemologies, though dominating ordinary educational thought are, in actual fact often hidden in the routine of educational strategies and practices and not necessarily known to the teachers who have them. But they do reflect much of the over-riding socio-economic relations of our late capitalistic world today and, apparently, do not evoke uncomfortable feelings and doubts.[10] Mirroring the world of buying and selling by commodifying knowledge,... it is small wonder that the trade of educational thinking between teacher and pupil, teacher and society, and pupil and society looks like a market where adjustment strategies and aggressive competition are more important than enlightened and critical forms of reasoning and clarity of thought.

This status of epistemologies in ordinary educational thought must not be accepted as a modern *condition* of educational thought.

References

1. George Santayana, 1955, p. 6.
2. John Dewey, 1939, p. 241. See to this also:

   "To claim that intelligence is a better method than its alternatives, authority, imitation, caprice and ignorance, prejudice and passion, is hardly an excessive claim. These procedures have been tried and have worked their will. The result is not such as to make it clear that the method of intelligence, the use of science in criticizing and recreating the casual goods of nature into intentional and conclusive goods of art, the union of knowledge and values in production, is not worth trying. There be those to whom it is treason to think of philosophy as the critical method of developing criticism. But this conception of philosophy also waits to be tried, and the trial which shall approve or condemn lies in the eventual issue. The import of such knowledge as we have acquired and such experience as has been quickened by thought is to evoke and justify the trial." (Ibid., p. 274).
3. George Herbert Mead, 2 1969, p. 322.
4. N.K. Devaraja, 1993, p. 167.
5. As N.K. Devaraja, 1993, thinks so (p. 168).
6. By replacing Waismann's "language" with "knowledge" teachers would be welcomed to clarify meaning in a process in grammar:

   "By grammar we mean everything about language which can be fixed before language is applied. We contrast the grammar with the actual application of language. (...) In short, grammar includes all the enormous number of conventions which, nowhere expressly formulated, are presupposed in the understanding of everyday language. It is precisely the formulating and bringing to consciousness of these tacit conventions, the discovery of this complicated network of rules which constitutes the philosophical clarifications of our ideas." (F. Waismann, 1971, pp. 13-14)
7. See to this the definition of knowledge and its explanation by V.G. Childe, 1956, pp. 54-55: "Knowledge is to be an ideal reproduction of the external world serviceable for co-operative action thereon." He explains this as follows: "(1) 'Is to be' because no science claims exhaustive knowledge and also because knowledge as here understood can never be complete or final. (2) 'Ideal' that is 'in heads', but not in your head or mine alone...but 'in the heads of

society'. It was superfluous to include the word 'social' in the definition since its implication in 'ideal' has already been demonstrated... I sometimes use 'conceptual' as equivalent to 'ideal.' (3) Re*production* is used to emphasize that knowers do not just receive impressions and passively reflect them as mirrors do. They produce a pattern from them. (4) Yet *re*produce, inasmuch as the elements and patterns are given in experience and derived from the external world. It must, therefore, somehow correspond to that world. (5) External world because (mainly) outside heads. I use this term as the counterpart of ideal in preference to real to avoid suggesting that ideas are unreal. But where there is no ambiguity, I shall say 'reality' for variety. (6) 'Serviceable in action' is just a reassertion of the 'practical character' of knowledge as deduced on historical grounds...(7) All distinctively human action is co-operative."

8. Mortimer J. Adler, 1985, p. 89.
9. A.V. Kelly, [3]1989, p. 8: "Curriculum studies...is seen...as a critical, analytical exploration of the curriculum as a totality, a theoretical/conceptual and practical/empirical examination of all the many dimensions of the curriculum debate and or curriculum planning, a critical evaluation of curriculum theories and practices, and a form of inquiry which goes far beyond considerations of mere methodology and transcends both particular subject specialisms and particular age ranges."
10. Kwame Anthony Appiah (1991, pp. 336-357) speaks of trade in epistemologies which depends upon the creation of a market for a particular type of knowledge.

2

Theory and Practice

Since we have introduced ordinary educational thought, it is now necessary to consider something which is *not* ordinary in thought, viz. *theory*.

To describe and judge something as 'ordinary' means to pose it against something which is more than ordinary. This something need not be of extraordinary or special quality, but it certainly should not be reactionary either. For, if it were reactionary, it would lose its appeal to something which is ideal. Ordinary educational thought is often reactionary because it has closed its doors to the intellectual ideals of openness and open-endedness; it also entails an element of resignation—a fait accompli of educational practice to which the teacher is resigned.

Ordinary educational thought represents the strong feeling that practice has to take precedence over theory. Once this feeling dominates a teacher's work, his thoughts, outlook and personality will be further shaped and encroached by pedagogical matters of convenience; these matters generally sound plausible and even laudable to the educational establishment of parents, administrators, and even pupils. Matters of this kind are, for instance, the notions that only a teacher is right, that there has to be a fixed timetable, that there has to be a best pupil in class, and that the evaluation of a pupil's achievement has to be demonstrated on a fixed scale. Reinforced by positive reactions of the educational establishment, teachers come to like their down-to-earth attitudes and do rationalize them a bit further if necessary. They do this obviously not for their own mental sanity but for their apparent rightness about how to deal with pupils and knowledge. In the end they use them regularly and have thus arrived at the grand road to pedagogical routine, euphemistically called 'experience'. All that follows then are mechanistic reactions to occurrences neatly labelled for all seasons.

It is still a myth why it seems to be inevitable in many a teacher's professional life to equate routine with experience. I have observed myself slipping into it and have seen it done so by scores of others. Only in a few of our profession does the deficit of theory finally lead to a dissatisfaction with our own practice. The majority of us remain through a whole professional life impatient with, and indifferent towards, theory which we know would force us to become critical of our ordinary educational thought. That is why we argue that theory would not help us in teaching better; in actual fact, however, we are afraid that we would hate to question many of our set beliefs and practices.

Being ruled by ordinary educational thought, teachers have resigned themselves to unsatisfactory conditions even if they are able to explain them perfectly well. The power of the ordinary not subjected to inquiry has taken over. A teacher's circulatory argumentation—*x* works fine in condition *y*, that is why condition *y* is right or good—is the classic expression of reactionary, non-theoretical educational thought.

The end product of such a way of thinking is that reason has degenerated to being a mere instrument, and reality has dissolved into objecthood. Objects continue to be investigated but not our knowledge *of* them which would demand a critique of the reason that aspires to know objects. That is why Kant, as one of many philosophers, did not provide a 'doctrine' but a 'propaedeutics'.[1] At this stage, teachers exemplify an extreme form of 'empiricist epistemology' within their set up of epistemologies in which a rigid methodology of knowledge is internalized in the relation of knowing to the known. The critical project of teaching, "according to which things are not what they seem to be and abstract concepts. . . and other categories not available to the senses are endowed with the status of the real, seems in eclipse".[2]

Contrary to some trends in postmodern thought, viz. to regard what is in use also as right and good and to justify the 'other' (situation or person) always as justifiable[3], I maintain that educational practices are only successful when they are set against standards of reflection (and not reaction). Reflection has to turn critical when faced with practice, simply for the reason that there are no educational strategies, techniques or skills which could be raised to a standard of perfection, a 'doctrine'. Flaws and imperfections are part of any practice. They can, however, be identified by reflective educational thought, put under the scrutiny of controlled action and fed back to critical thought. This would then be 'the more' than the ordinary: it would be a framework for bridging theory and practice and qualify as a Kantian 'propaedeutics'.

By doing so, we can agree with W. Carr and his 'historically sensitive' concept of practice in education which he posits very close to the Aristotelian concept of praxis to escape the instrumental thrust of recent educational theory and practice:

> A 'practice ', then, is always the achievement of a tradition and it is only by submitting to its authority that practitioners can begin to acquire the practical knowledge and standards of excellence by means of which their own practical competence can be judged...But the authoritative nature of a tradition does not make it immune to criticism. The practical knowledge made available through tradition is not simply reproduced; it is also constantly re-interpreted and revised through dialogue and discussion about how to pursue the practical goods which constitute the tradition...It is precisely because it embodies this process of critical reconstruction that a tradition evolves and changes rather than remains static or fixed. When the ethical aims of a practice are officially deemed to be either uncontentious or impervious to rational discussion, the notions of practical knowledge and tradition will tend to be used in a wholly negative way...[4]

The question which now arises is, what to propose in this framework for teachers' epistemologies? We may remember not to regard these epistemologies as reactions to, or reflections of technical problems in the specialized theory of knowledge, and we certainly do not want them to continue as reactionary sets of beliefs. A different and more promising method would be to accept them as *attempts to teach within histories of ideas...* As to this, two points have to be discussed first, namely, what are histories of ideas and how do they become parts of teaching and learning?

To teach *within* histories of ideas is not to teach the subject History of Ideas. The latter is an academic discipline, rather well-defined and divided into elements of subject-matter and methodology—it represents objectified knowledge in areas of civilizations. Following A.O. Lovejoy, we can argue that the subject History of Ideas contributes to the ways to "understand ourselves better by understanding the ways in which we have evolved, which largely means to understand the manner in which we have come over time, to hold the ideas that we do".[5] Our suggestion to teach *within histories of ideas* can surely gain from the basic discussion in the subject History of Ideas[6] by, for example, becoming more sensitive towards thinking of the past as a problem and a challenge. Our proposal is, however, occupied with the *outcome* of thinking, the knowing of something. For this, it need not be 'enacted' or 're-enacted', even if this were possible, in any thought that has produced and reconstructed knowledge.

Teaching *within histories of ideas* consists of the endeavour to come to terms with the past of any subject, not so much in an historical or a social order but in an attempt to comprehend as much as possible of what has been discovered, thought or experienced, or experimented in any given subject-matter. To be exposed to this attempt, which is the process of acquiring knowledge, is to enter the vastness of a subject and of human knowledge. No mechanical storing device will ever be able to cover it fully because human knowledge is in a constant process of change; stock-taking of it is already obsolete the moment it is done. New methods of exploration and analysis are being continuously discovered and alter even past knowledge. That is why our exposure to knowledge should not only be attached to the rules of how to deal with the products of knowledge, but should also be open to the subtleties of process. We shall then find that many of our ideas have already been thought, that many of our fleeting impressions have already surfaced somewhere else.

This deja vu may, on the one hand, generate a feeling of being so awestruck that one loses any initiative to build upon one's precursors in thought and discovery and to be, instead, satisfied with faithful recording and repetitions. On the other hand, there could be the reaction to prefer to ignore these histories knowing fully well that one can do so only because one has been educated in the mould of them, and that it is pointless to think through them because they are a fact of one's own existence. But even the contrary could occur and we would become curious to go beyond these histories and to surpass them at any cost—which, then, is another way of forgetting them. Or there may be the pragmatic be-happy status, viz. in accepting them in full as firm bedrocks of progress in knowledge formation where Euclidian geometry has to be rediscovered and the origins of the First World War be relived just for the educational purpose of learning.

Histories of ideas, whatever the reactions by teachers, are dominating teachers' epistemologies by either cementing organized sets of justified beliefs or by sowing the seeds of reflection and scepticism as to knowledge production and transmission. Here again we have to say that this process is partly known to teachers and is partly taking part in their subconscious. Whatever the degree of identification or rejection with histories of ideas, whatever they have aroused or not, they have assisted in shaping any teacher's knowledge of something. Even the seemingly unhistorical fact of the falling apple which led to the theory of gravitation is based on histories of ideas, viz. that things *can fall*, that one is *able to see* this, and that one is *able to think* about it (tempting me to think that Descartes's *cogito ergo sum* was not so bad after all). The qualities of 'falling', 'seeing', and 'thinking' have histories of capabilities related to how human beings have generalized over time what these words mean; and they have specific histories in relation to the individual who has discovered their meanings for himself. The three concepts would not be taken for granted without a dip into those histories, since they are "abstracted out of ideas about the use of words, and based upon internal shapes of language patterns".[7]

In sum, we may consider in a general sense histories of ideas in educational thought as acts of knowing something. In doing so, knowing is always understood as something which has a past: the moment we know that 1 + 1 = 2 or that a painting on the wall is square we have gone through observations, calculations and thoughts which are a thing of the past at the time of arriving at a conclusion or a proof. It is not the object alone which has a history but also the act of perception, the act of dealing with the object which has to be seen in the light of the past. In knowing means and ends we are also acknowledging ideas of the past as right, workable, useful as in our example that numbers can be added and angles can be measured and that we can give names to these results. This acknowledging does not curb the potential of critical reflection; rather it is being enhanced by including a dimension we tend to overlook in an understanding of knowledge which is too often only future-oriented. Once we have acknowledged that behind every object and every act to grasp this object there are histories of ideas, the more we shall be able to look for them, to use them, and—eventually—to enjoy them.

At this point, histories of ideas can potentially become assets for our educational practices because they may enrich them by creating a higher confidence towards knowing, adding so to the realization of Kant's Enlightenment demand "dare to know".[8]

The acceptance of histories of ideas behind virtually everything that we do and think and have acquired is not an all or nothing affair in which a right or wrong, a good or bad is to be swallowed. It is the ability to set standards through knowing; the deeper the knowing, the finer and firmer the standards. This is again not in a categorical fixing of right or wrong but in a greater subtleness of questioning what could be right or wrong. Once these standards are in place, even an otherwise average teacher will feel, after some time, how he has grown in transferring ideas and their histories to his pupils, nota bene again histories of objects *and* histories of understanding them. His pupils will have learned to cherish these standards, if found genuine, more than some cheaply populist fashions and tricks which are not uncommon in pedagogical routines.

A teacher in this mould has replaced the old subject-centred conception of reason with something in which reason is to be construed as the internalization of social norms. This thing has to be gained anew every time and cannot be trusted as a built-in component of the human self.[9]

The chief reason for the acceptance of standards by pupils is that with standards come humility and firmness. To *know* a word, a formula, a musical tone, or a moral means is the same as *to have made it one's own*. From then on auxiliaries become secondary and techniques of convenience do not matter that much anymore. Whether taught in a Socratic or Deweyian way, whether with the help of a piece of chalk or a computer, whether in a metropolitan state-of-the-art university or a village school—histories of ideas provide means for knowing the object and knowing how to know the object with a continuum whose ontological attributes go far beyond the knowing of facts. Then knowing has become being and has turned from a tedious and often hated exercise or a means of survival into an activity which has changed into a source of joy. We are sometimes aware of this joy, but we are not always conscious that knowing is the source of it. It is perhaps the art of teaching to help pupils become aware of this source.

We may now assert that epistemologies in reflective educational thought can be employed to trace histories of ideas in any subject-matter and in any method. Along our definition in the earlier section, we still maintain that epistemologies continue to function as providers of what is considered right and good by teachers, but they would do so in reflective educational thought in a more critical and organized manner. A precondition for this is that the building of epistemologies has to become an open process of knowing and not-knowing; any teacher would have to undergo such a process in a kind of psychoanalysis of knowing, a catharsis of the problem what do I, as a teacher, know, how can I know this, where are my limits of perceiving and comprehending, and what shall I claim should be learned by pupils. The discussion of these questions may result in an understanding that we should do much less in class than even a single textbook with its accumulated knowledge wants us to do, or much more, depending upon the level of comprehension we can expect in us and our pupils.

Furthermore, the results of a catharsis of knowing may also give us confidence in working with fundamentals of knowing (basic concepts and basic methods) which in turn would enable us to give reasons for right and good in our epistemologies . At this point, we would be entitled to call a teacher a 'social epistemologist', recognizing, however, that our intention is not so much "resolution" (as it is in the case of S. Fuller[10]) but the deepening of the social and intellectual process of knowing in reflection of educational process. And with this we would have made a first step to help build bridges between educational practice and theory in affirming and demonstrating new disciplinary boundaries and authorities which are meant to shift from teacher to pupil and vice versa.[11]

I should like now to advance the thesis that *a modern condition of reflective educational thought is represented in its task of generating continuous dialogues between theory and practice, by making these dialogues the vehicles for essentialiazing and contextualizing educational thought and practice.*

To approach the argumentation of this thesis, I first take recourse to two kinds of concepts which are both found in theory and practice. By analyzing them in their capacities as theory-constitutive and practice-constitutive we may be able to form a materialist base for our concern to use teachers' epistemologies in a reflective manner. By a materialist claim I mean that the mental is mentally constituted, as opposed to being identical with the material.

The concept in the realm of theory I should like to call *essential* and that in the realm of practice *contextual*.

The explanation of what is understood by an essential and a contextual is very much influenced by asking the question, what does it mean to say *a* or *b* in educational language. But here again we must not be satisfied with definition alone: standards set by history, values and norms and expressed through language have to be taken into account too. Without them we would be lost in empty or positivistic thought. But it also means that we have to leave a strict empirical level and adopt a more speculative attitude. This attitude must, however, not be mistaken for idealism, it is rather a reflection on human nature which cannot be restricted to objectivistic approaches only. If this were possible, we would not have had the millenia-old conflict between the ideal and the humanistic. That people have seriously thought and still do so that the ideal has to be striven for and that this is more a matter of mind than of empirical data is reason enough that it represents a powerful facet of human nature. To deny this would be a-historical. And if we did so, we were not justified in understanding education as the belief in the improvement of the human condition through the process of enlightenment and emancipation.

To distinguish between two kinds of concepts, even if they are *represented by the same word* as in the case of an essential and a contextual, seems to put us in the unenviable position of being confused. But this is precisely the position we are trying to explain in much that follows in this inquiry. Is it not the struggle with confusion which is the beginning of philosophizing, and is this in turn not the aim of all good education? The explanation will trace a more social than a purely epistemological argumentation. This procedure is characterized by taking into account relations to time, space and, what I should like to call echoing Habermas, "lifeworld".[12]

Essentials and contextuals can represent, and often are represented by, exactly the same word, but only in the realm of ideas or abstractions, and never in the realm of proper nouns. A proper noun we would change by adding a qualification—if we wanted to say for instance, that a chair is yellow or comfortable. This we would not do with, say, justice, if we wanted to qualify it. Justice would remain justice in whatever qualification we think of it. Certainly an uncomfortable chair would also remain a chair, but not to the degree justice remains justice whether we mean by it, for example, constitutional or extra-constitutional justice.

This same word, however, does, not mean the same at different times, in different places and in different locations. Since human activities are temporal acts in different locations and cultures, the same word has to have a different meaning for different people. But this rather well-known and innumerably discussed truism should not be employed here as a line of argumentation, lest it would lead as to a kind of relativism I do not have in mind to defend at all. What I want to put forward is the idea that the same word can also mean different things for the *same person*.

A person never lives in the same time. As soon as one physical moment is over, another moment follows, as soon as one thought has crossed his mind, another crosses his mind or if one sentiment has been stirred up in him it will the succeeded by another. Thus, a person is always in the process of leaving or entering time.

A person is never in the same place either; though this is physically possible, it is not conceivable mentally: the impact of a sunset on him is different all the time throughout the time of the sun setting, i.e., the object that is changing in space, in our example the earth imaged in the sun, is directing a spatial variation in a person as well though he may continue sitting at the same spot. His mind, if receptive to a sunset, travels with the object and is therefore in different spaces. The idea of beauty, for example, would have travelled with these times and spaces.

But what about a still object? Even here I should like to argue that space is changing mentally in a person [illegible] the sense that a still object, say, a book in front of me, is not actually still because it is permanently creating images for me. These images vary from moment to moment, from maybe an object of beauty because I see its perfect print, to one of boredom because I do not see the book move. In other words, my perspectives of the book vary from thought-moment to thought-moment. Therefore, we can never consider time and space constant and unchanging in relation to us as persons.

If time and space are not constant in our perception, then it is but obvious that our lifeworlds, steeped in traditions and customs and determined by norms and values of a multitude of practical actions, are also in constant change. Let us call a lifeworld a culturally fixed behaviour which is, in turn, always trying to change its cultural matrix. This has to lead us to believe that time and space induce cultural change on the one hand, and cultural changes are the causes for variations in time and space on the other. From that it is easy, indeed, to see why a word not only can but must in most cases mean different things to the same person at, seemingly, the same time and in the same location. The imprint of a word on the mind is so strong that it has the power to change the mind's impression of time and space. The lifeworld, only a crude presentation of the mind, has no chance but to react.

But this is only half the picture for the material conditions of the lifeworld. The social skills and practices, and the intuitive knowledge constituting a lifeworld enable a person to deal with a situation by directing the mind to focus *in relation to* time and space. If, for instance, the book is not being placed in front of me or if I am not in the right spot to observe a sunset, then these presentations would not have happened to me—but others would, with a different impact on my mind. There cannot, however, be any doubt whatsoever to regard physical restrictions like hunger and pain, sentiments like love and suffering, and social relationships whose expressions may range from compassion to power as the most dominating elements in construing one's lifeworld. That is why intuitive knowledge is not just there but is made; it has emerged from experience and left imprints which we use for 'intuitive' spontaneous reactions.

These reactions are, as rational actions, part of 'culture' in the way Max Weber and Jurgen Habermas understand it. For them, culture is not beyond consciousness and rational expression, as it is for Michel Foucault and other post-structuralists for whom it is a code or some other invariant structure, but always something which people *do*, whether in deed or thought.[13] In Habermas, consciousness is historically and socially situated in discourse which invites to possible different outcomes.

Let us now apply an essentialist and contextualist concept which is the same word with different meanings to the same person—in different roles though. We take 'justice' as our example.

First, justice can be presented as a result of legal-philosophical thought which has surely a great relevance to many parts of our life but only when we are faced with a practical situation where we have to use it or to think about it. As a value per se for, say, education, it is meaningless as long as it is stored as a looming value or a vague idea which is hardly taken care of. Its existence is only a dormant one, a canon of authority, good to be there, pleasing for our feelings towards justice in general, and, satisfied with its essentialist character, giving 'some ' value in its ideational role to ideas.

Let us now think, second, of justice as an idea a teacher wants to use to justify his procedures to promote pupils from the weaker sections of society. His is an expression of active sympathy that implies to enter into dialogues in the face of what he thinks is right and just. The means he adopts for this depends a lot on how he is going to assess the situation of the lifeworld of his pupils as well as his own in relation to the former. An element of calculation may creep into his thought, tactics will be contemplated, sympathy has to be transferred into proper actions against an indifferent, if not hostile, environment. Justice thus presents itself differently to him compared to the legal-philosophical thought which he, the teacher, has taught, the minute before rather mechanically, in class in relation to, say, the French Revolution. (Certainly, the French Revolution could also evoke a contextualist response from him depending on his understanding of the topic and the way of teaching it.)

In the legal philosopher, justice assumes the quality of an essential, in the activist teacher it has been employed in the form of a contextual. In both, justice is understood as a value attached to an idea. Thus, even though the legal philosopher and the activist teacher are the same person, it does not prevent them/him from employing justice at one time as an essential and as a contextual at another.

Educational thought (theory) is signified by operations with essentials whereas educational practices (practice) need the directives of the field which produces the contextual, or else practices would miss the dimensions of time, space and lifeworld it depends upon.

Despite upholding our claim that these three dimensions play a role in both, the word as an essential and as a contextual, we have nevertheless to stress the point that there is a degree of abstraction on both levels. On the level of an essential, i.e., while essentializing a word, the dimensions are less pronounced and less specific than on the level of a contextual and are to be produced in the most general philosophical deliberations. Complementary to this, on the level of a contextual, i.e., while contextualizing a word, we prefer to be down-to-earth and quick to point out which hurdles and obstacles have to overcome in order to make contextuals function; on this level, the three dimensions of time, space and lifeworld play therefore an important role.

To sum up, an essential represents an idea (often formulated as an explicit value as in the case of justice) which is thought necessary for the purposeful functioning of education. A contextual also represents an idea but one which is nearer to the real life of a pupil and a teacher; it is also nearer to the real nature of a thing as presented to a teacher and a pupil since this thing has been explored, experienced, reflected upon, and finally been made part of one's social awareness. Essential and contextual which are copresent in an educational idea and practice are, though distinct, mutually implicative.

In the preceding as well as in the subsequent elaborations I use only for practical, i.e., illustrative reasons the argument that we are dealing with *two* concepts. Pedagogically, they are constructs of mind in order to make an explanation more plausible. As so often in practical thought on education and teaching, we are less precise than we, philosophically, ought to be. I have adopted this fundamental approach of a teacher even in this inquiry at various places but cannot hope to get away with it unnoticed.

That is why I should like to state here that whenever I refer to essentials and contextuals not the concept itself does not change but (only) the *understanding of it*. Let us take *C* for concept and *u* for understanding of it. Through the process of contextualization we create *Cu1, Cu2, Cu3,* and so forth. *C* never changes, *u* does. It is certainly a kind of arbitrary demarcation to say, for instance, that after *Cu3* a concept as an essential has changed into a concept as a contextual. On the other hand, these changes cannot be denied, they are observable and henceforth labelable. The changes may occur in whatever manner, gradually, over time of, say, between *Cu7* and *Cu12* or abrupt, eventually already at *Cu2*. These changes are real. And if a teacher can be made conscious of this transformation, he will be able to add to his repertoire of strategies for pedagogical encounters. He will like to do so simply for the reason that changes in the sensibility of concepts recognized by him would enhance his sensibility towards the fine tuning of knowledge production. Once he has realized that knowledge is not so clear and neat as he has been made to believe, he will want to design different methods to fathom and teach these changes. The somewhat crude distinctions of concepts into essentials and contextual may help him then in his endeavour.

For further clarification let us think of another example, this time of one which has no obvious value character. The example is the word to 'know', Considered as an essential, it is foundational, i.e., it gives a fundamental direction to education, viz. that its purpose is to make pupils knowledgeable Why do we believe in the word and its direction? The answer is fairly simple: we believe in it because we think that it is universally believed in and therefore, right to do so. But is this rightness truth? Certainly not, because rightness is dependent on human agreement, truth need not be. An essential needs the agreement (and hence it is not a universal which would need truth[14]). And in terms of to 'know' to claim agreement is fairly easy because it holds so much of commonsense that hardly anyone would doubt it as a commendable activity. Have not scores of teachers, pupils and parents subscribed to the rightness of to 'know' ! But here lies also the danger of stopping thinking and not questioning the 'what' and 'how' of to 'know', and leaving these questions to specialists in curriculum design and planners in administration. Their collected wisdom is then handed down in textbooks and syllabi. This does not mean that an essential has turned into a contextual. By selecting and cataloguing its 'whats' and 'hows' we have undoubtedly enriched an essential but we have not touched it directly.

Contextualizing is *not mere application* but a discussion of the foundational belief into what to 'know' *is* in a particular educational practice whether, for example, it is an *awareness* of injustice or an *ability* to write, and so forth. The rightness of to 'know' as a contextual becomes more pronounced when we attempt to understand the 'deep structure' of an idea. We attempt this because we intend to be congruent, i.e., to combine the congruence potential of both an essential and a contextual. There is always a push-and-pull effect in a word to go from the 'I shall be just' to the 'I am just'. (That as teachers we often try to ignore this push-and-pull effect is a different matter, usually a matter of convenience, of comfort neither to be pushed nor pulled.)

Is it then not possible to theorize with contextuals only? No, it is not. Normally contexts can be fully determined and saturated so that we apply ourselves within them habitually in the right way. This, however, is changed when we are talking of specific contexts (e.g., in critical thought or scientific research). Then the net of context is so extremely wide that we have difficulties to include all of them—which would be necessary to arrive at rightness. To recur back to essentials is therefore not only a normative necessity but also a necessity to provide some meaningful—either full, minimal or projective—understanding.[15]

Since the most precise thought cannot achieve fullness of comprehension, we have to refer to 'experience' as some source of knowledge in the shift from essential to contextual and vice versa. It is consciousness, the datum of experience or the act of experiencing content, which is the reason for change of a fictitious purity of an essential and the emergence of a contextual. Let us think of our example 'justice'. The moment we are thinking of it, we have a perception of what it is. It is not something formless, something non-existing; neither is it something objective. Each one of us, while thinking of it, creates an image of justice which is different from each other because there is already an understanding of meaning as soon as we think. That means an essential is from its inception or conception as thought already conscientisized or, in other words, historically determined—though this image of an idea is in a simple imagination and thought rather dormant, hidden in a latent kind of non-use. As soon as we activate it (further) it becomes conscientisized (further) and gradually assumes the nature and role of a contextual. In this we are either conscious (reflective educational thought) or not conscious (ordinary educational thought) of its historically determined shifting content. In the former, we have, after a long enough process of conscientization, created a new essential.

For example, the character of 'justice' has changed for us depending on whether we have studied it as part of the Indian Freedom Struggle, where it has to be studied in conjunction with non-violence as a crucial way to achieve freedom, or the Algerian Revolution, where we have to take into account the practice of violence in its aim to drive out the French. It has changed whether we have read M.K. Gandhi or Frantz Fanon. In the former, we may well think of justice as a kind of fairness[16] in which one should never use evil means, whereas the latter is addressed clearly as a form of justice which might be called a single-purpose one which justifies on its way every means to achieve its purpose.

In both these concepts we find a mixture of historical and utopian thought though the latter is stronger in a contextual because of its nature of taking side. This quality and its exuberance open up "alternatives for actions and margins of possibility that push beyond historical continuities". May be it is not too far-fetched to draw a parallel for the formation of essentials and contextuals in what Habermas says about general political thought, namely, that in fact "modern time consciousness has opened up a horizon in which utopian thought fuses with historical thought" and in which "political thought becomes charged with utopian energies but at the same time this excess of expectations is to be controlled by the conservative counterweight of historical experience".[17] I suppose we are allowed to see essentials *and* contextuals together as such a controlling force.

And certainly their changes would have something to do with the truth values of presuppositions, be they logical or pragmatic. An essential would allude more to the former, a contextual more to the second in which appropriateness of context would dominate. Logical presuppositions are rather easily specifiable, not so however pragmatic presuppositions which are, nevertheless, just as fundamental for our understanding of meaning in specific situations out of which we form new meanings:

> While the 'truth values' of logical presuppositions are determined by relations within sentences or between contiguous sentences, the 'truth values' of pragmatic presuppositions are determined by the level of discourse—specifically the juncture between them. In a field of competing discourses all claiming to be languages of truth, this pragmatic 'truth value' becomes inevitable since it serves as the fundamental presupposition of the entire discourse—its readers must recognize its special status as the privileged mode of expression.[18]

Out of the above, we may conclude that there are also two modes of pedagogical thought, the essentialist and contextualist. A mode of thought is the clubbing together of strands of directives which we need as signposts for reasons of morality and mental health. To exist morally and mentally needs the search for orientation. (That is the reason why religions have always been so powerful in man's life; they have often proved to be reliable providers of satisfaction or doubt. That they carry with them a slave-mentality is another matter.) By a mode of pedagogical thought we understand a specific trend of seeing and answering pedagogical questions. While confronted with these questions we are approaching them with preconceived notions of how answers could be gained, which kinds of answers would be appropriate for our purpose, and how these answers would help us justify our basic ideas of knowledge and education. But we also have preconceived notions concerning the questions which may or may not be asked, which may or may not be forced to be discussed in classrooms.

In an essentialist mode of thought we would expect answers to be gained by analysing questions from a philosophical angle. That means we would be probably satisfied with general answers since they may serve our philosophical quest best. We would probably accept completeness, consistency, comprehensiveness and coherence as criteria for claims about the nature of the world, the nature of human beings, and the nature of knowledge[19] And we would attach a high epistemological value to the methods with which we would have questions to be answered and formulated so that our basic ideas of education can be grounded on, say, a rational foundation in a perhaps Russellian sense.

In a contextualist mode we would accept answers to be found by putting together a number of facts from related experiences. We would hope to elicit answers of a highly practical nature since they would go along with our search through experience. These answers would then, quite naturally, support our arguments on the experiential nature of education in a maybe Deweyian sense.[20] And we would always feel challenged to counter essentials as a-historical categories, which celebrate too much of imagery, and which would hide the real interests of those using them.[21]

The essentialist mode of thought is characterized by four trends: it is more future- than past-oriented (but not in the sense of utopian); it has, because of this, a weaker historical rooting; it is not prepared to regularly use social analysis; and it is usually in favour of a fixed canon of knowledge.

Since the essentialist mode deals with general concepts, it is future-oriented. These concepts have waited to be used, to be activated, and there is no reluctance on our part to avail of them. In such a mode we would often ask the questions, how can this concept be understood, and when should it be used? We would try to assess the potential use of the concept for future action. In this sense, essentials are used as aims or goals of education. These goals or aims are an anticipation of what we shall do in future and what we want to achieve in future. But it is not utopian in the sense that it vigorously pushes us to new horizons—its future-orientation operates in a measured conservatism. For example, if 'justice' is being aimed at, it tells us that we want to practise it because we find it good, but it does not commit us to a clear qualification of justice.

Besides being declared to be desired, essentials are also understood as concepts which signify, at the same time, a principle *and* a technique: to be just *and* to aim at justice respectively. The use of essentials by teachers, always aimed at others, also demonstrates a desire of something which not only they want to do and to achieve, but also what they want others, their pupils, to do and to achieve. Inexactitude and incertitude of the essentialist mode of thought are mainly due to this future-orientation in which balanced belonging may count more than robust analysis and wild dreams.

If so strongly future-oriented, it must come as no surprise that the essentialist mode regards the historical method as being less important. There is certainly the acceptance of 'history' as the great provider of experience which can come only from a looking back, but this past-orientation as a source of experience and ideas has done its duty as soon as an essential has been conceptualized and gained a place in a set of normative ideas. Thereafter, 'history' and its method may vanish into obscurity—unless the essentialist thinker bears in mind that the historical process he has undergone of what can be called a change from individual knowledge to social knowledge[22] is an ongoing one which, as a matter of fact, has not stopped with him while conceptualizing, and that in reality he has arrived at a provisional essential only.

We are tempted to regard the process of conceptualization as closed once we feel safe in knowledge, i.e., as soon as we have generalized knowledge. In education, this may lead finally to complacency towards knowledge production and construction since generalized knowledge of the kind of '1 + 1 = 2', 'the French Revolution began in 1789', and 'India is a developing country' gives no room for questioning the bases of this knowledge; it is simply accepted as true or right and is thus contributing to a confirmation of the value of the essentialist mode of thought, in this example concerning the essential/contextual to 'know'. This mode is then considered a safe haven, an abode of stability for teachers who cannot imagine to be involved in the conceptualization of essentials over and over again—which would be accepting and practising the historical method. With this they often shut the doors to new experiences and ideas.

Out of this follows that neither historically nor presently is the essentialist mode of thought driven to employ social analysis as a tool of inquiry. There is the occasional attempt to analyse social reality by looking back or looking ahead, but a social analysis is not legitimized as an essential to produce knowledge. Instead, it is felt that ever so driven, the essentialist mode would precisely lose what it claims to be its greatest strength: its general character, [illegible] its universal aims, its generalizibility even its possible appeal to all, [illegible] in adverse conditions when, for instance, [illegible] education is hardly possible in a just or non-violent way because of oppression, exploitation, or simple mental laziness. But not going deep into social problems brought up by any knowledge which is understood as an ongoing conceptualization, the essentialist mode of thought can, though, continue to promise hope to each and everyone at one time or the other. Contrary to religious essentials which work only in tandem with the strict following of rituals, an essentialist pedagogical mode of thought does not insist on a beaten path to salvation and enlightenment. Hence, hope is joined by declamations for freedom to act, decide and choose.

Once it has been proven again and again as being successful, advocates of the essentialist mode will not cease to point out its high value. In education, we daily face the case of a curriculum which should be flexible as to new conditions, needs and desires. To ascertain them, social analyses would be needed. But since they are not considered necessary, the essentialist mode is satisfied with 'tradition' (not 'history' which has a method, whereas 'tradition' has not). A tradition is less likely to be changed because people who adhere to it are convinced of its truth value, both logical and pragmatic, and continue to believe in it unequivocally and irrespective of circumstances. Such a high truth value has been attributed in education to knowledge presented in a fixed canon. This fixed canon represents an essentialist mode with stability beyond the belief in the rightness and righteousness of an essential. It resembles here *sabda*, the belief in authority as the source of knowledge found in classical Indian epistemology as a suitable method.[23] A fixed canon of knowledge appears as a promise for hope and freedom, as path tried out by generations before and proven successful as in the case of some American colleges where the 'Great Books' are being taught in order to cover about 2300 years of (Western) intellectual history.[24] In this context of a fixed canon, K. Kumar distinguishes between a "received" and a "dynamic" perspective on the curriculum. By "received" he means that curriculum decisions are derived from an "a priori view of knowledge", whereas in a "dynamic" perspective, knowledge is placed in a "sociological context and inquires into its legitimacy".[25]

The contextualist mode of thought in education is characterized by one main trend, viz. the grappling with social and educational reality, its historical roots, and with as many socializing factors as possible. That is why in this mode we are ready to accept changes in knowledge and hence are open to new curricula. The level of long-term satisfaction is lower than in the essentialist mode because there is no resting on former laurels. Everything is understood to have an impact on forming new ideas and concepts. This everything is, however, strongest in our thought of the past. Whenever we think, we also always think 'back', so to say we are relating new thoughts to old thoughts, new impressions to old ones, we are comparing the present and a possible future with the past: thinking has then become another name of discourse.[26]

'History' in such an environment is the contextual pillar for a contextualist mode. Present political, social, economic and cultural problems have to be measured against the 'what-could-be'. The future 'could-be' can only be ascertained when out of an analysis of the past, new ideas emerge and try to clarify this 'could-be'. In our example of 'justice', we would surely attempt to take stock of what has and what has not been worked out in legal thought of the past; furthermore, we would try to find out how people before us have implemented justice.

The contextualist mode of thought regards itself as part of a methodological continuum ranging back to the beginning of humankind and forth to possible results of our actions and thinking. A curriculum is, therefore, less important as a standardized entity: stability is not sought in fixtures but in conscious approaches to change and the willingness to support it. Thus we would be keen to expand the concept of justice by trying it out in new situations, by fighting established forms of judging and doing, and by using it for the justification of actions and thoughts we deem good.

A modern condition of educational thought depends on *both* these modes of thought, the essentialist and the contextualist. They together can deliver, to education, organized epistemologies which promise to work for stability *and* change, resistance *and* risk-taking.

On the one hand, both these methods are involved in the construction of epistemologies which work for the establishing of an essential network of guiding ideas and values, creating a feeling of hope on its way, promoting the power of human nature, balancing the trends in human beings to do good and evil, and generating optimism by looking forward. On the other hand, they are contributing to epistemologies which are supporting in the minds of teachers and pupils a healthy scepticism against authority, existing knowledge, and values which have not been examined fully. Their tentative answers point to a scientific temperament conducive to the desire for change.

Combined in such a holistic endeavour, essentialist and contextualist pedagogical modes of thought form a background of epistemologies which Erich Fromm found common in Sigmund Freud and Karl Marx and which I should like to accept for any form of education. They are characterized by accepting everything human (but discarding those traits which lead to unhappiness), doubting obsolete ways of dealing with people and problems, believing in the liberating power of truth, and perceiving reality dialectically.[27] Thus doubt (about traditional knowledge), the power of truth and humanism could form the matrix for an epistemological ethic in which the procedure would be as important as the quality of content; in other words, where the means would be no less important than the ends.

If teachers can be convinced that both these modes of pedagogical thought should work together, then they will be able to create a dialogic relationship between theory and practice. Reflective educational thought, combined modes of thought, and an epistemological ethic are the foundations of a circle which can establish a permanent dialogue between theory and practice. Nothing short of this should be the goal of a theory of education which strives for a humanism that is to reconcile the known with the unknown.

References

1. Murray Bookchin, 1996, p. 47.
2. See to this Stanley Arnowitz, 1977, p. 770, who describes this process with regard to students in college. I agree with him that probably students are prone to this 'empiricist epistemology', but perhaps so because many teachers do model their teaching on the same. To the 'empiricist' position see the postulates of N.V. Banerjee, 1958, pp. 34-46: 1. Knowledge is a congnitive relational phenomenon between subject and object. 2. Things outside of us are knowable or intelligible. 3. The object known exists independently as a physical thing forming part of the spatio-temporal world. 4. Our knowledge of things is direct and immediate. 5. Our knowledge is essentially cognitive judgment.
3. See to this Oyvind Osterud's (1996) severe attack on postmodernism. On its terminology he writes: "At the surface it is disclosing itself in trendy terminology, with politics as *discourse*, the world as *text*, verbal depiction as *narrative*, narrative as construction of *meaning* and *meaning* as *construction* of reality, and—for sure—any foe or antagonist image is simply the *Other*." (p. 385) See also Dipankar Gupta who thinks that the signposts of postmodernism are to view all distinctions and definitions with extreme suspicion which leads to a dispersal and deferral of meaning by accepting the "multivocality and fictional character of concepts" (p. 394). He adds that postmodern scholarship "displays a rather uniform disregard for theory, axiomatic logic and demonstrable coherence" but would attempt "to use all the literary, poetic and metaphoric options available in order to deliver *depth* experiences". (p. 396).
4. Wilfred Carr, 1987, p. 170; see also the rejoinder by Ruth Jonathan, 1987.
5. As summarized by Preston King in his introduction to Preston King (ed.), 1983, p. 8.
6. For instance, about the two positions "that all knowledge is of the present, and alternatively that it is all of the past...On the one hand, to understand past ideas, we are enjoined to think them through ourselves, to bring them to life, perhaps to 'enact' or 're-enact' them. On the other hand, such understanding, we are told, may only be achieved by ceasing to think as we do now, by shedding present outlooks, by removing ourselves to remote times, by appreciating how different *our* thought is from *theirs*, by reconstructing their contexts rather than assume any constancy or continuity between earlier and contemporaty ways of thinking." (Ibid., p. 4)

7. Robert M.W. Dixon, 1966, p. 175.
8. In the opening paragraph of his famous essay "What is Enlightenment?" (1784), Immanuel Kant, 1977, p. 132.
9. This is what Richard Rorty (1989) sees as a move in Habermas and Wilfred Sellars (p. 62).
10. See to this one of the reviews of a review symposium on Steve Fuller (William Keith, 1995, p. 489): "Fuller does three basic things for any given topic; he identifies the impasse and the relevant parties in the dispute, suggests why they all need to resolve the impasse, and proposes a resolution based in social epistemology. (Note that for Fuller, a 'resolution' may be a view that shares little with the views of the controversants and may bypass their disagreements rather than 'resolve' them. Those who are sentimental about their traditions need not apply.) Thus the social epistemologist is set up as the mediator to controversies about knowledge production. Unlike Quine's epistemological 'referee' (blowing the whistle on transgressions of methodological rules) or the harsh judge of traditional foundationalist epistemologies (who sentences knowledge claims to oblivion if they do not meet positivist burdens of proof), the social epistemologist is a mutual participant whose authority derives mainly from skill in the rhetoric of intellectual dispute resolution rather than from privileged access to knowledge or method."
11. See to this the introduction to the essay collection *Between Borders: Pedagogy and the Politics of Cultural Studies*, edited by Henry Giroux and Peter McLaren, quoted in Bell Hooks, 1994, p. 129.
12. Quoted in Detlef Horster/Willem van Reijen, 1992, p. 21, from Jurgen Habermas *The Theory of Communicative Action*, vol. 2, Boston: Beacon, 1984, p. 35: Lifeworld "consists of individual skills, the intuitive knowledge of *how* one deals with a situation; and from socially acquired practices, the intuitive knowledge of what one can rely on in a situation, not less than, in a trivial sense, the underlying convictions. "Jeremy J. Shapiro, the translator of Habermas's *Toward a Rational Society* (1971), explains 'lifeworld' ('Lebenswelt') as a term which "refers to the irreducible fabric of meanings in everyday life, in which the meanings of specialized, constructed, or formalized languages are embedded." (p. VIII)
13. See to Habermas's conceptualization of 'culture' Michael Pusey, 1987, pp. 198-204.
14. Sympathizing with Foucault that truth "has to be understood as a system of ordered procedures for the production, distribution and operation of statements", and that truth "is linked in a circular

relation with systems of power which produce and sustain it" (as quoted in Ian Hacking, 1989, p. 35), I nevertheless maintain that there is perhaps truth we do not always know, or truth which need not be related to power structures, or truth which may exist beyond the purview of our cosmology.

15. Charles Spinosa/Hubert L. Dreyfus, 1996, p. 751.
16. John Rawls, 1973. See to this also Vinit Haksar, 1986.
17. Jurgen Habermas, 1989, p. 49
18. Jim Collins, 1989, p. 81, referring to arguments by Edward Keenan ("Two Types of Presupposition in Natural Language", in: Charles Filmore/D. Terence Langendon, eds. *Studies in Linguistic Semantics*, New York, 1971).
19. Charles Spinosa/Hubert L. Dreyfus, 1996, pp. 738-739: Essentialism "makes two interlocking claims, one about the nature of the world and one about the nature of knowledge. Roughly, the world consists of things that fall into kinds or types. Any knowledge consists of recognizing and relating those types and determining which type each thing is an instance of. More specifically, essentialism claims that the intelligibility of things, people, institutions, selves, and so forth requires that there be one complete, consistent, comprehensive, and coherent description of reality. *Completeness* requires that every entity (but not every mixture of entities) be an instantiation of at least one context-independent type (or essence). This requirement is supposed to satisfy our intuition that we have knowledge of things because we know their types (that is, their essences). *Consistency* requires that two types can only apply to the same entity if the entity can be characterized by all the defining features of both types without contradiction. This requirement satisfies the intuition that a set of types must, on the one hand, enable us, for instance, to encounter antiques, tables, and antique tables while, on the other hand, enabling us to encounter clouds and emotions but not a cloud emotion, *Comprehensiveness* requires that there be an ultimate, inclusive set of types. This requirement satisfies the intuition that every intelligible type must fit in with the rest. *Coherence* requires that there be a principle that determines why any particular type belongs to the ultimate set. This requirement satisfies the intuition that there must be some order accounting for the consistency within the set of types. Essentialists allow that much empirical and transcendental work needs to be done in order to bring out the right types and their principle of coherence. In the end, where intelligibility is concerned, the essentialist must deal with seemingly contradictory principles of coherence by showing how one supersedes the others."

20. See to this John Dewey, 1964.
21. Edward Said, 1995; see pp. 331-334 of the Afterword to this edition.
22. See to this Bertrand Russell, 1992, pp. 17-22.
23. See e.g. Debiprasad Chattopadhyaya,[6] 1986, p. 179.
24. Take for example, St. John's College in Maryland. Though the list of books has been under continued review since 1937, the changes are within accepted norms from where "an understanding of the fundamental problems that human beings have to face.. at all times" can be gained: "The first year is devoted to Greek authors and their pioneering understanding of the liberal arts; the second year contains books from the Roman, medieval and Renaissance periods; the third year has books of the seventeenth and eighteenth centuries, most of which were written in modern languages; the fourth year brings the reading into the nineteenth and twentieth centuries." (St. John's College: *Catalog 1996-1997*, p. 22) I have to admit that I share the views of the College that these books are "both timeless and timely" and that they can "change our minds, move our hearts, and touch our spirits". And the statement of the programme adds convincingly that these books "speak to us in more than one way. In raising the persisting human questions, they lend themselves to different interpretations that reveal a variety of independent and yet complementary meanings. And, while seeking the truth, they please us as works of art with a clarity and a beauty that reflect their intrinsic intelligibility. They are, therefore, properly called great, whether they are epic poems or political treatises, and whether their subject matter is scientific, historical or philosophical. They are also linked together, for each of them is introduced, supported or criticized by the others. In that sense they converse with each other. they draw the readers to take part, within the limits of their abilities, in a large and continuing conversation." (Ibid., p. 6). On the other hand, I would suggest a college of this nature give students a greater opportunity to search for themselves for Great Books and to choose them according to their own individual needs. Maybe that is too much to ask from an undergraduate course, but at least a beginning could be made to loosen the canon a bit.
25. Krishna Kumar, 1992, p. 20.
26. George Santayana 1955, p. 291.
27. Erich From, vol. IX, 1989, pp. 46-49. In this, these epistemologies are remarkably similar to M.N. Roy's radical humanism with its axiology of freedom, truth, and knowledge. See to this M.N. Roy, 1981 p. 53.

3

Pedagogical Essentialism and Contextualism

The problem I wish to discuss in this section is how essentialism and contextualism can and should go together in the educational thought of the same person.

As said above, in ordinary educational thought we tend to turn more to the essentialist mode of thought. The reason for this is not necessarily a strong belief in essential properties without which an object cannot exist, as one would ascertain from a classical understanding of essentialism[1], but a kind of instinctive desire for security, stability and steadfastness. In ordinary educational thought, essentialism is, therefore, used as a means for survival which is seen in continuity rather than in change.

The teaching profession is susceptible to this conservatism because teachers tend to think that only when they are backed by a totally predictable environment can they bear the demands of the pupils and the knowledge claims inherent in a curriculum. That is why a change in their relationships to pupils towards a more open and equal one and openness towards the construction of new or different knowledge are virtually anathema for most of them. We have to deal today with the profession as an agency which has been diluted from a force of societal change to a force which promotes existing and traditional knowledge. The desire to do good, not necessarily to an overall system of values but to a system of political and/or social rule, strengthens a teacher's will to lie low.

But why are demands made by pupils and claims by knowledge so threatening to teachers? Should one not think that both their aims, namely, stability and change, present exactly the challenge we need in good education? Why are so many in the teaching community so indifferent to stability *and* change? We are here not searching for an easy explanation as we could find, for example, in a teacher's daily fears how to manage classes well and how to maintain discipline. These fears are certainly widespread and are for quite a few teachers genuine reasons not to dare contemplate change or to take any risk in relationships and contents. But there is a deeper reason for this contempt of change. And this may be found in the attitude of a teacher towards the individuation of the growth of a pupil in relation to his specific need for, and understanding of, a particular knowledge.

This individuation towards knowledge is said to be achieved through the development of language against public references and may thus, at best, follow an anti-foundationalist course. Anti-foundationalism is the doctrine which asserts

> that guarantees of knowledge are not provided by any foundations outside ourselves or inherent in some transcendental ego. If there are any such guarantees—and on that there is controversy—they can only inhere within our own linguistic practices. But if our linguistic practices are given for individuals and (are) intrinsically social, it follows that knowledge is only made possible, if possible at all, by the linguistic practices of whole communities, rather than those of pre-social individuals. And since these social practices are plural and variable and thus contingent, they cannot be taught as foundations. If language speaks man, there are no foundations of knowledge.[2]

If that be true (and I assume that many of us in the profession 'feel' like that without formulating it in the same complex way), then the education of a pupil conscious of himself and the knowledge to be acquired takes place in the narrow space of learning the right word for the right thing, not knowing precisely whether the language of his knowledge really represents the world. Teachers know this dilemma and 'solve' it easily by a) referring to accumulated knowledge of the past, preferably in neatly and logically fabricated statements and definitions, and b) telling pupils that the right knowledge for their world is with them, their teachers. But a teacher also knows that such a way of teaching is not to follow his ideal (which he has hidden from his pupils) and that his dictate is finally contributing to an incomplete education which is not giving the pupil a chance to discover the right word for the right thing on his own. This is not a maxim of good education discovered by the advocates of child-centredness but an age-old precept of many an ancient culture. Note, for example, what an ideal teacher was at the time of Confucius:

> (I)n his teaching the superior man guides his students but does not pull them along; he urges them to go forward and does not suppress them; he opens the way, but does not take them to the place. Guiding without pulling makes the process of learning gentle; urging without suppressing makes the process of learning easy; and opening the way without leading the students to the place makes them think for themselves. Now if the process of learning is made gentle and easy and the students are encouraged to think for themselves, we may call the man a good teacher.[3]

Being such a teacher would mean to accept the risk of experimenting and to come up eventually with the wrong word for the right thing or the right word for the wrong thing. Deep down teachers know that this is how it should be in their classes since they know in principle that pupils should go through their own process of discovery as often as possible and wherever appropriate. They also do admit that knowledge (as the outcome of a series of right beliefs) should be constructed with the active participation of the pupil, and that it should be continuously reconstructed in discourse.

But despite knowing this and being concerned with the well-being of the pupil, they are not willing to grant this freedom without safety strings attached to it. It is not so much the nearly insurmountable mountain of practical difficulties like large classes and inadequate resources which prevents them from committing themselves to discursive freedom of knowledge construction, rather it is the more existential fear of losing their grip over pupils which leads to an almost instinctive repudiation of this freedom. They think if they allowed this freedom without attaching strings of control, their status of a knower, *the* knower of some thing—for example, that a table is not a chair and cannot be named a chair or the belief that to love thy neighbour is good and should not be replaced with the doubt 'But what if he is a nasty fellow, may I then slap him?'—would be diminished. Their love for power in class demonstrated to their pupils by knowing the right word would be challenged irrevocably if they granted them the full discovery of the right word. Pupils would become knowers all of a sudden and teachers would be *also*-knowers. And consequently they are afraid that their power would fade away.

Furthermore, there is among teachers a widespread uneasiness about their most significant tool—language. On the one hand, they glorify it as the vehicle of knowledge transmission and the guarantee of power, on the other they know that it creates "*what counts* as reality"[4], i.e., objective knowledge as appearance, not what *is* reality, and that they would have to be careful about the distinctions in ordinary speech, i.e., ordinary use of language which determines widely what knowledge is supposed to be.

The practice of education is about standards, setting them, maintaining them, and assessing them. In all these activities language is involved as its main connecting force. Language connects our ideas and thoughts for setting standards, orders our actions for maintaining them, and gives a framework for assessing them. It is closely related to thought insofar as it could not exist without thought, as is also the case vice versa. Thought is the great ordering force for all actions in an educational encounter and language is its convener.

Teachers are aware that the language of setting standards is the thought process or 'inner speech' they use constantly in selecting, transmitting and evaluating knowledge. This 'inner speech' cannot be studied objectively, not even by the thinker himself. We shall never know what is really happening during our thinking, but something of it is expressed in language and assumes a linguistic and factual appearance in the open. But language inadvertently also represses something of what we have thought, and as teachers we are aware of this as well. Thus, since language is unable to give a full picture of what and how we have thought, language is used by us to create an illusion of completeness which makes us forget fast that it is never the sum total of our thinking, but that it per se has turned into a smokescreen to hide truth. This incompleteness of his knowledge is known to every teacher, and the reason why it is hardly ever admitted is again the fear to lose power.

But should teachers not be happy about these possible states of also-knowers and incomplete knowers? Should they not be satisfied with the role of a knower who becomes therefore gradually less important for his pupils? Should they not be glad about the development of pupils into independent young men and women? To be honest, they are not. Since they have been brought up in the tradition of a pedagogical hierarchy with distinctive knowers of complete knowledge (teachers) and non-knowers (pupils) and having suffered from once being a knower-in-part (as a pupil), they do not want to be deprived of the status of now being a knower. And they want to be known as a knower which can only be achieved by exercising power in the form of transmitting knowledge which is unquestioned. This status allows for selecting the knowledge they think plausible and valuable for attaining aims and objectives, but this status, upheld over generations, also tempts them to simplify knowledge and to refer to acknowledged, received knowledge or a canon. Whatever trend they follow, it is they who decide (often in a willing collusion with the political powers to be who, much too often, base their motivation also on a will to power). The consequences of either trend are to be found in social reactions, first in expected reverence for the knower, and second in perpetuating the status of a knower.

But there are surely many teachers who feel that this is an intolerable situation, and that is why they have tried to find an elegant way out of this dilemma: they offer a compromise and define their new role as that of a facilitator of the pupil's search for individuation and his discovery of knowledge. This can be rightly called "Pseudo-Freirean" as has been done, amongst others, by K. Kumar who blames these teachers for converting "dialogue" into the search for correct answers, "predetermined by the programme planner and provided to the teacher normally through a teacher's guide. In effect, dialogue thus becomes a subtle form of 'banking'", and he adds that those teachers would use the Freirean term "dialogue" but would apply it "interchangeably with 'discussion'."[5] This means that they can feel good about themselves because they have gained in progressive image and have at the same time shed the burden of an authoritarian preacher; but mainly they have retained their status of the final arbiter as to knowledge.

A teacher's authority is the outcome of a peculiar mix of the three categories Max Weber has classified for a legitimation of power: the traditional, the rational-legal or bureaucratic, and the charismatic which involves attachment to the person of a powerful individual leader.[6] Nurturing this mixture by either attaching it to syllabus, knowledge or relationship, teachers contribute strongly to the 'save school' movement, i.e., institutionalized education, and to calm down the fear in any society that radical individuation would perhaps lead to the abolition of all related institutions of education and research and would leave a society with nothing but educational anarchy which may become the springboard for political anarchy then. Teachers are the last who would want this to happen, and so they are prepared, if at all, to work only for measured reform which does not affect them and their society's security and safety. The essentialist mode of thought seems to promise to ordinary educational thought just this conservative potential.

But the essentialist mode of thought in ordinary educational thought operates with a conception of an essential which is doubtful as an aid to the reconstruction of knowledge. The wrong view attached to all essential lies in the misleading understanding of what a concept is. It is *not* the straightforward and clean comprehension of the underlying idea behind the fact or belief for which it is taken in ordinary educational thought (and ordinary thought as such). It is not the unambiguous and crystal clear understanding of something. It is certainly a fact or belief comprehended by a person but not necessarily, if at all, purely. Since values enter into the formation of all concepts and thus become part of the content of concepts, there cannot be consistency in the meaning of concepts.[7]

No concept can be purely comprehended because it would entail the possibility of a pure subject, a pure object, and a pure way of comprehending. In claiming conceptualization as pure we would have to strive for a completely valueless, disinterested and detached person and comprehension. This seems to be impossible with the subject of comprehension being man, the object of comprehension being a creation of man, and the act of comprehension being an act trying to connect two incompletes.

We may in Wittgensteinian terms agree that "being socialized into a culture includes knowing how to apply our concepts in *normal* situations"[8] —but who determines where the normal ends and the special begins? D.W. Hamlyn is equally careful when he opines that "(t)o have a concept is to have a *certain* form of understanding" and that "a condition of fully understanding a concept is that one should be able to apply it in *relevant* and *suitable* instances".[9] To conceptualize is not only to abstract or to create a network of abstractions; it must touch reality at some point and is therefore open to interpretation.

Purity of comprehension and purity of an object would symbolize something like absolute truth, all ideal we may be longing for, but a goal which is unachievable in education. Purity would be a certainty, again an impossibility which we cannot overcome. Pure comprehension would be finally a comprehension without content, but any concept is by its very existence a concept *of* and, therefore, a concept *with* regard to some thing, i.e., to a content.

Within our materialistic outlook, we have to reject the Cartesian consciousness as the self's essential quality and hence maintain that in the sentence 'I am conscious of something' the subject exists only at the moment at which it is conscious, the object exists only at the moment at which it is brought to the consciousness of some subject, and consciousness also exists only at the moment at which it occurs.[10] So even the elusive consciousness should not be considered as a means of creating purity; it is as bound to time, space, and content as any other thought.

Content prevents us precisely from comprehending a concept as pure, absolute or certain but does allow us, however fleetingly, to arrive at an immanently contextualized essential. The (thought of the) essential ' Justice' generates in US an image of what justice ought to be and, thus, momentarily is in our image. For example, we could imagine 'justice' as a contractualist argument and agreement to mutual toleration, or a consquentialist argument in which we agree that the consequences of acting tolerantly are better than those of acting intolerantly, or as an argument about respect for parsons which provides a moral agreement for toleration.[11]

We can imagine 'justice' as an experiment with these and other forms in relation to educational problems like to enforce compulsory education or to structure a time-table in such a way that each pupil can choose the courses he wants to study, or attend to the learning needs of every pupil. But all these examples are based on nonlegal criteria of 'justice'. The examples appeal to a particular quality, that is integrity, and express a meaning or justice' that appears closer to moral rightness than fairness. Many sore distinctions could be made, but I hope to have made the point clear. We are left with the conclusion that the generation of images cannot be 'doubled, which means it cannot occur at the same time twice in the game person, and it cannot occur in two people identically, and thus precludes the possibility of an identical image in either one person or two persons . But only such an identical image would be pure, certain, an truthful.

Instead the process of comprehension is full of impurities, uncertainties, and tentative truths - nothing bad in itself and as a matter of fact quite normal and unavoidable. We on would have to accept that it just leaves us with the option to improve the impure, the uncertain and the tentative. And this is precisely what education aims at. Education is finally to benefit from such a realistic approach which is oriented towards continuity and growth and not towards a fixed process and a rigid product.

Another quality which makes conceptualization unfit for arriving at an essential devoid of content is the latter's active character. A concept is not only an idea, it is also an 'active' one inasmuch as it is contributing to its change when being the object of thought. Since there is no identical thinking of any object but only one thinking at a time by any one person - in other words: there is only one encounter between subject and object at any given time - the object not only *appears* different in the next encounter but *is* different. It is neither a physical change in the thought of an object which has made it different, nor is it its commonsense or basic understanding of its content which has done 80 , rather it is the *action of looking at it* that makes an object part of this action.

In the action of looking at it, an object begs for clarification, explanation or definition; once it hag been dealt with in such a manner, it is to be transferred into a concept. To have arrived at this stage, viz, the conceptualization of an object, is, however, not the end of the road. Once conceptualized, a concept does not qualify as an object for being forever the same concept. On the contrary, as soon as the concept has been formed, it has turned also into another object ready for the next thought by the same person to be explored. That is why a concept is never 'still'. It would be more honest to understand it as some thing which is in a constant flux between the state of an object and the state of a concept, the object being the idea which has been thought of just before, and the concept being the idea after the beginning of a thought.

For practical purpose, we may now be allowed to infer from this flux in which a concept is all the time that some basic core or it may be understood as an essential. The outer layers of this core, added in a continual process of conceptualization, which is finally contextualization, make the essential open to change, and the inherent elements in an essential to allow change .

Here I should like to point out that an essential is not a universal but a combination of a universal (e.g. 'justiceness' and *a* particular (e.g. 'justice') conceptualized by a in a situation *b*, which gives an essential a common property *only when perceived*; in a universal, instead, the common property exists whether perceived or not, in "simplicity and eternity"[12]. An essential is perhaps something like a trope which is an 'abstract' particular, viz.

> an instance of a property occurring at a particular place and time, such as the color of this book or this page. the whiteness of this page and the whiteness of the previous page are two distinct tropes, identical neiter with the universal whiteness that is instantiated in both pages, nor with the page itself; although the whiteness of this page cannot exist independently of this gage, this page could be dyed by some other color.[13]

A contextual is, accordingly, not a particular but perhaps a combination of a particular and a universal. It is some thing which we know much legs directly and less intuitively, and we have to labour to get a sense of it. In either ease (essential = universal + particular; contextual - particular + universal) it is the first item of these combinations which is a kind of determinant of the concept in question. This may lead us to the conclusion that at one point in time an essential has turned into something more contextual, and a contextual into something more essential at another. To follow this line of thought would be practicing reflective educational thought which is still, let us emphasize this again, dealing with 'impure' and uncertain conceptualisation of tentative truths. We should be under no illusion that pure comprehension is possible. If we were, we would pave the way for ordinary educational thought to take over. The attempt to cultivate reflective educational thought, however, would soon convince us that there is no interest-free and desire-free concept because its formation is always attached to a new thought and with it to a new motif.

We can now speak of a teacher who is inclined to accept and practice his profession in the essentialist reflective mode as a person who tends to systematize his ideas in what I should like to call pedagogical essentialism, leaving another type of teacher who is bent upon to use a reflective constextualist mode of thought to systematize his ideas in pedagogical contextualism. Neither does the former abolutize essentials in his epistemologies, nor does the latter absolutize contextuals in his epistemologies. We may assume that both types are determined to respond meaningfully to problems in education by employing one of the two combination as the more appropriate as and when problems of application of thought arise.

Pedagogical essentialism is here denoted as the process of the construction of a grand educational design, as a 'Grand Narrative', which is to demonstrate the universally affirmed core of concepts and their layers of contexts. We may deduce that, complementary to this (but not instead of it), pedagogical contextualism is to be considered as a continuous pedagogic reflection on ideas and practices pertaining to a specific human condition.[14]

The essentialist grand educational design and the contextualist continuous pedagogic reflection together can lead to good education and to a "combination of freedom and learning that all teachers seek and few ever find"[15] and which would force us to answer these questions over and over again: how much of freedom do I grant myself as a teacher in order to be able to work with epistemologies which are in a constant flux, and how much of freedom do I offer to pupils in order to let them grow into, and experiment with, all sorts of epistemologies?

Why is it so difficult for a teacher to solve this problem of freedom and learning? I may offer the following explanation. It is so difficult because it is not easy for them to accept and promote a *circle* of freedom and learning in which freedom is considered a precondition of learning, and in which learning in turn makes teachers more sensitive for freedom. This reasonableness does not convince many teachers because it goes against the traditional *hierarchy* of learning and freedom to which we usually tend to adhere: something has to be on the top, and another thing has to be at the bottom.

We are endowed with a zest for comparison: one has to be better than the other, stronger, faster, and so forth. To be able to compete well is one of the main sources of this thinking. The more we are focused on competition, the more hierarchical do we think. Political and economic thought and practices have contributed to this domination of competition at the expense of cooperation and have meanwhile pervaded nearly all spheres of our life: the emotional relationship between parent and child, the educational between teacher and pupil, and the social between friend and friend. Hierarchical thinking outnumbers spiral thinking by far, and one casualty, amongst others, is a possibly balanced relationship between freedom and learning. I call this relationship 'possibly balanced' because there is controversy whether these two do not contradict each other. The very desire to learn something does restrict one's freedom to learn something else. It does so in such a way that over time the manner of choosing becomes automatized and hierarchical in a syllabus. And, thus, any syllabus is the (necessary?) restriction to freedom.

To overcome this, at least partly, to make it less rigid, would need design and reflection stimulated by great ideas. Without great ideas there would be no ideals, and any guidance would be downgraded to a mere utilitarian attempt. Here we consider an essential in its social function of an ideal which sets standards (in its philosophic explanation of a word it describes how the word is to be used and what it means; in its metaphysical function it constructs a whole world by itself). Though these functions are at times closely intertwined (the social being determined by theoretical speculations, but also becoming sometimes so powerful that the theoretical simply vanishes), they have to be kept apart for the sake of clarity. Continuous pedagogic reflection can be the means to reconcile these functions, turning the ideal into the real and making the real more palatable for the ideal.

There is probably no educational doctrine which has not been caught between the three, leaving it often enough to a rather arbitrary choice whether the doctrine will end up in epistemologies of ordinary or reflective educational thought. The former would soon cease to exist as a continuous reflection and be satisfied with the status quo providing a sort of stability to educational practices which, on the surface, makes it so convincing for parents and others who see school education from outside. The latter would accept the 'duty' to understand the 'continuous' as *permanent* and by this help education to become a fascinating but somewhat unstable adventure leading to many eyebrows raised in the educational environment of administrators, parents or others who have an interest in public education as a perpetuating force in and for society.

To understand the roles of essential and contextual—or to use a Habermasian label: ideas we have in consideration of the lifeworld—will help a teacher tackle the humanistic nature of education. It culminates in the question whether education is the object of thought of something practised in an institution. Since we always have to see and discover the individual pupil in education, it would not be just to take his role lightly as simply a part of a group (even if we cannot forget completely our hidden agenda).

But what does it mean to keep him in mind? Nothing but to perceive him as a human being who, like us, loves, suffers, despairs, rejoices, and so forth. If however, we prefer to address him as part of a crowd, we are seduced into a false understanding of neutrality and objectivity which makes us believe that everyone before or around us is there only to grasp our knowledge in the same way as we do and to use it in a like manner. Yet educational reality is different. In a classroom we have as many perceptions as we have pupils, and unifying their perceptions and behaviour is only a way of making it easier for us to control them. Against this, rigorous attention to the one person in a crowd is a more reliable foundation of humanistic education.

Now what is this humanistic nature of education? In a nutshell we say define it as a relationship between person and person in order to be able to continue to live as a person—free, rational and moral. This includes the formation in the fullest manner of all the faculties of man so that he is able to utilize them for his personal joy and social responsibility. The humanistic nature of education is deeply entrenched in the individual and social, or in the care for himself and the love for others. It has to provide him with skills to fulfil these tasks, and with principles to justify them. To strike this balance is to resort to elements of art and not only of thought. Any technique in the transfer and assimilation of knowledge is dependent upon communication the unavoidable presupposition of which is the guarantee for dialectical learning.

If really nothing fixed is required in education according to John Dewey[16], at least one stable element is a must: *communication.* Even in the highest esoteric form of self-education do we communicate with ourselves or an imagined absolute. Communication is not only a set of techniques but through its potential of dialectics, also a principle. To communicate is always considered good (like in our earlier explanation of to 'know'), but it becomes better when it is a domination-free communication. And the principle and technique of balance form the humanistic core of education; they strike a balance between the personal and the social. This may be realized by searching in the educational process for the space between reason and experience and not for one of the two alone. When a person knows how to rely on both reason and experience and the something in-between the two, then he will he able to contribute to the education of all his faculties. And maybe this is exactly the artistic in education.

Let me try to explain this 'in-between' reason and experience in education. It can be perhaps understood as the *outcome* of the 'applied'. While learning that '1 + 1 = 2' we use reason to explain it (by explaining the function of adding) and experience to make it clearer (by referring to examples around the pupil). Even if the operation has been perfectly understood by the pupil, teaching and learning must not stop here though. A pupil should be encouraged to apply his new knowledge, if not in practice then at least in imagination. The more he does so, the more he will learn how much knowledge affects his life in the personal as well as in the social domain. In order for a pupil, to distinguish between the two domains, teachers are held responsible to create opportunities to distinguish the two domains so that a pupil can become aware of himself as a product of the two, but also how far he could possibly create the social. To do so is, of course, also based on reason, experience, and the in-between, but the whole process should be gradually left more and more to the pupil and less to the teacher whose prime task is to explain the technicalities of operations. A pupil should be invited to the widest possible choice of applications, he should be allowed to fantasize, to dream, but also to calculate coolly his chances. It is not surprising to see how such artistic enterprise is then being created in education. The pupil has finally accepted and proved himself the constructor of part of his knowledge.

But perhaps the most important point of the humanistic nature of education is that it is aimed at critique and emancipation. The critical acumen of a pupil is gradually to be deepened and strengthened to enable him to understand his place in the world and, on account of this, try to change it if found wanted. This creates conflicts which are the salt of educational practices; they may be conflicts of opinion, conflicts of knowledge domination, or conflicts in personal and social relationships. They cannot be willed away but have to be addressed in a process which may finally lead to autonomy. (It is interesting to speculate on the notion whether harmony, the golden mean, or the equilibrium are in actual fact the killers of autonomy.) This is all very well as regards an individualistic remedy which would primarily focus on change in us, but how about the social emancipation of the subsystem education. This could only be achieved by an autonomy that

> must be construed as a social product with our motivations and goals arising from legitimated or discouraged by surrounding social structures and the emotional attachment we find in them. This being so, the exercise of autonomy—once developed—must be construed as a *social* good which creates the context of its further development and exercise in others. Were we to construct our concept of autonomy as a socially located, inter-subjective *social* value we would not only begin the reconstruction of a theory of liberal education for all, but also address what is beginning to be acknowledged as a theoretical impasse for political philosophy.[17]

Critique is not only critique of the other but also demands of us reasonable self-critique of attitudes, interests and desires. We have to single these out because the three of them are the driving forces of what we do and whether we are satisfied or not with our actions. The very possibility of being dissatisfied should encourage us to regard ourselves not only as a subject but also as an object, i.e., we *are* not only dissatisfied but we are also a *source for* dissatisfaction, individually as well as socially.

How shall we then deal with a situation in which we are full of resentment and discontent, either individually or socially induced? Even at the danger of sounding too optimistic, it should be possible by reverting to reasoning and experiencing by using one's mind more than one's emotions. Together with critiquing, these two form an emancipated person whose sentiments, thoughts and actions are all tied to communication, inter or inter, which makes in turn these forms of learning possible. Reasoning without communicating would end in wordless exercises, experiencing without communicating would be an unreflective exercise, critiquing without communicating would never be just, and emancipating without communicating would be to cook something without food. A loss in communication would result in an imbalance between the individual and the social and thereby put in doubt an important function and foundation of the humanistic nature or education.

This balance between the personal and the social in education can only be fully achieved in the dialectical process of transforming a subject into an object, and an object into a subject: 'I' into 'justice', and 'justice' into 'I'. In the former we attempt to not accept 'justice' as, for example, the task of a state which in its ideas and rules has also to be normatized by the same state, but we would be actively involved in 'justice', say, in our classrooms. This in turn will then have a direct impact on our conception of 'justice'. In the former, we may well hope to create enough essentials, in the latter we are sure to produce a sufficient number of contextuals to contribute to a unity (not identity[18]) of theory and practice. In both procedures, we would also address the questionable dichotomy of subject and object by discussing that qualities in their existential occurrences are neither purely objective nor subjective.

Communication is chiefly language, and in the educational situation it is used to influence the behaviour of others and to express thoughts. All fairly complex thoughts require words.[19] I trust that the greatest importance of language is that we can use it for the description of things first of all, not as they are but as they are perceived. Thus we combine the social function of language (something is being described to convey information/ meaning to others) with its individual function (information and meaning are largely dependent on one's perception). Hence language constructs epistemologically essentials and contextuals never only on one plane: 'justice' as an essential is more dominated by a description and less so by a perception; in a contextual it is just the other way round. But these are not their exclusive functions; they may start with them but need not follow them through. They can mix them freely and they do so, so that an observer is often not quite sure where the demarcations are to be located.

We see that description and perception will often go together; they should be treated as the two sides of a coin and should enable teachers (and pupils) to develop at any time some form of communication which I shall like to call 'engaged qualitative thought', i.e., our capacity for interpreting our environment. This capacity can be used for seeking qualities in a situation or context. These qualities, because of their pervasiveness in the whole experienced situation, exert a regulative influence on the direction of the development of thought but are also engaged in shaping and constructing values.[20] This engaged qualitative thought can then be used to help recognize where opportunities and limits are located in a person and a society, be they equality of chances, justice for all, limited intelligence, or adverse economic conditions. A humanistic education would place engaged qualitative thought in the centre of its theory and practice so that teachers and pupils who engage in this reflective exercise delineated above arrive at a balance in their social and academic relationship.

References

1. Antony Flew 1979, p. 104.
2. Nigel Blake, 1996, p. 221.
3. Lin Yutang, 1966, p. 247.

4. John Searle in Bryan Magee, 1992, p. 156.
5. Krishna Kumar, 1989, p. 87.
6. Cf. to this Paul Edwards (ed.), 1967, p. 283. See also Max Weber, 1962, pp. 81-83.
7. See to this Christopher G.A. Bryant, 1955, on Max Weber on concepts and value relevance (pp. 20-24).
8. Charles Spinosa/Hubert L. Dreyfus, 1996, p. 745. (emphasis mine)
9. D.W. Hamlyn, 1983, p. 110, pp. 126-127.
10. Nikunja Vihari Banerjee, 1958, p. 51.
11. Partha Chatterjee, 1997, p. 256.
12. See to this the essay "Some Aspects of the 'Universal'" by Gopinath Bhattacharya in Gopinath Bhattacharya, 1989, 70-94, where he claims, beautifully executed, the reality of the objective Universal and its transcendence. I have, however, to admit that Bhattacharya would never subscribe to my conclusions that an essential is perhaps a combination of a universal and a particular, and that a contextual may be one of a particular and a universal (see below). These would be for him logical impossibilities. And rightly so. Neither would he agree to the possibility of a 'trope' (see below). I can only defend my approach as a struggle with pedagogical compulsions, and these can, unfortunately, never meet strict philosophical criteria. Maybe we are somewhat justified by referring to categorical analysis in Indian Realism (a school of thought also employed by Gopinath Bhattacharya in his essay on the universal) where besides definition and logical divisions in a second place, categories are explained not "in terms of more simple notions, since they cannot be analyzed or defined" anymore, but also in showing their "*interconnections*" and noting their "*similarities* and *dissimilarities*"(Pradyot Kumar Mukhopadhyay, 1984, p. 167, emphasis mine). These interconnections, similarities and dissimilarities soften the strict logical approach somewhat.
13. *The Cambridge Dictionary of Philosophy*, 1995, p. 811.
14. That is why I should like to relate pedagogical contextualism to what Hannah Arendt (1989) calls the "vita activa" designated by the three fundamental human activities of labour, work, and action (pp. 7-8). Correspondingly pedagogical essentialism would allude to the vita contemplativa.
15. This is how the daughter of Bertrand and Dora Russell described the achievement of her parents at Beacon Hill School between 1927 and

1934 when she attended the school: "My mother shared my father's belief in the value of knowledge, and both parents wanted us to have as much knowledge as possible, for our own good and humanity. They hoped to make it possible for us to acquire it without pain, through the encouragement of natural curiosity, but, where curiosity failed, they were prepared to use other inducements, rather than let us remain in ignorance. Here they parted company with other believers in progressive methods, and here they made their particular contribution to education, achieving that combination of freedom and learning that all teachers seek and few ever find." (Katherine Tait, [2]1996, p. 83) Clearly, the Russells' understanding and practice of child-centred education was not one which deteriorated into child neglect and did not help create a me-society, as we have noticed so often in other child-centred projects where the love of knowledge was seen less supreme.

16. See to this John P. Wynne, 1963, pp. 256-257.
17. Ruth Jonathan, 1995, p. 106.
18. Sundaraja Rajan, 1987, p. 5.
19. Bentrand Russell, 1992, p. 74.
20. For this, the central idea has been adopted from John Dewey's paper on "Qualitative Thought" (originally published in 1930) in John Dewey, 1960, pp. 176-198.

4

Essentialism and Contextualism vis-a-vis the Lifeworld

The most prominent aspect of the lifeworld is its nature of totality or "the taken for granted universe of daily social activity".[1] Our activities which include thought and action are continually directed by our conscious or unconscious assimilation of this totality. This assimilation takes place in the interplay of the three structural components of the lifeworld—culture, society and personality. According to Habermas, culture is the reservoir of knowledge from which people who communicate take their interpretations; society is the legitimate order out of which people who communicate take their security of social belonging and solidarity; and personality represents the competence to communicate and to maintain an identity. These structural components correspond to the reproduction processes of cultural reproduction, social integration and socialization.[2]

But in assimilation and reproduction we not only organize but also build up more totality in our lives. This can lead to a situation where we are not anymore willing to think of our life as fragmented and, hence, a life in which thought needs to be critiqued and improved but to be controlled all the time. While control contains some measure of reflection of structures and fragments, an ever-growing totality does not demand reflection and critique. Since totality is always present, we not only take it for granted but often stop thinking about it. This is supported by a growing feeling that corresponding with an increase in totality we are anyway unable to regard the totality of our lifeworld from outside ourselves for we cannot step 'into this outside' and, thus, cannot have an outside view of it. Even if we tried to do so, we would never 'reach' the outside; instead we would only expand the totality of our lifeworld. Hence our view of our lifeworld can only be biased.

This feeling of an acceptance of totality is significant for our thinking about pupils and teachers. Two questions have to be raised in this connection. First, if the totality of a lifeworld is so fixed, do we really have a chance to get it intentionally altered in another person; and second, if the answer to the first question is affirmative, how is the manipulation to be done—"in other words: does it make sense to educate and if yes, how?"[3]

I do not think that an answer to the first question should come out of an exclusively idealistic frame of mind in which the ability of the human mind is to construct and impose categories on the world, nor of an exclusively realistic one by referring only to outside systems which are imposed on us through tradition or convenience. Possible answers would then simply appeal to either individualistic and opportunistic preferences or to values education claims to transmit and the knowledge it conveys within a system. I should like to prefer an answer from a different point of view, perhaps by a more critical looking at what we mean by 'totality'.

Totality could be understood as an entity that is stagnant and stationary, not open to change, an entity that is not only taken for granted but also taken over as a monolithic universe. But this meaning cannot be defended because totality is in actual fact constantly changing. A totality is not a fixed entity with clear boundaries, inflexible and impenetrable. Instead, it is an entity which at its seams is in constant movement, in a constant flux by growing and shrinking without losing its character as a total for a person who has it. We continue to think of our life as a total of whatever happens to it, whether it goes through crises or happiness. We are convinced of its wholeness whether we still have a full life ahead of us or whether we are already old. It may be shattered by upheavals or lived in the quietude of a forest, life as a whole is represented by, and taking place in, a (total) lifeworld.

Viewed from inside, whatever affects our life, does not change the central nature of our totality which is manifested in a focus on our life, even when we are seemingly working for others in a Gandhian or Mother Teresa like style. Changes at the seam are then not a big deal; they are merely understood as reinforcements of the core. Owing to this focusedness on oneself, only extraordinarily broad-minded people in education are able to understand totality as a permanent challenge to critique themselves. For most of us the totality of lifeworld is a given fact, a fait-a-compile which is always right in its total existence whatever happens at its seams and whatever cosmetic corrections we are willing to allow.

We may argue that it is not the physical totality which is unchangeable—I maintain though that this physical totality can also be changed at any time—but it is the casting of judgments on our totality which is as rigid as any monistic fanaticism. Hence a teacher would do well not to think in the first place of educating a pupil in order to have a direct impact on his lifeworld (by presenting him with a standardized set of knowledge) but to concentrate on an understanding of why and how a pupil has or has not arrived at his judgments and values, e.g., that 'justice' is good. This understanding should take into account reasons a pupil has construed over time only in his mind and reasons which have had a direct impact on him from outside, be they educationally-intentional or not.

Having arrived at this stage, we would be in a position from where we could identify and discuss entry points into the totality of a pupil's lifeworld. We would preferably use dramatic instances which have occurred in his life in order to come back to his judgments and values. These dramatic instances could be as harmless as 'It was good that I was caught when I stole some apples from our neighbour's garden' or as crucial as 'But it was not necessary for my father to punish me for this by beating me severely'. But we would also confront the pupil with past knowledge as to practical justice and ideas about justice.

An analysis of one's values and judgments does not alter the totality of a person's lifeworld per se but can surely start the process of inaugurating movements at its seams which might open avenues to discuss the core of becoming and being.

Entry points to totality are to be used by teachers to make education not just an exercise in the provision of information. The more the lifeworld of both teacher and pupil can be penetrated, the more meaningful becomes the former's education, provided the teacher can strike a balance between the two major pedagogical modes of thought. A successful penetration is, however, only achieved when the teacher is able to make it clear to the pupil that he himself has gone through this procedure regularly and is still ready to do so if needed. Pupils should gradually become aware that to question the totality of a lifeworld of another person, e.g., the teacher's, is also their right. The ongoing story of penetration must, however, not become a battleground for any mode of thought to gain supremacy. But their struggle can be used as an effort to coordinate and to cooperate in the task of clarification.

It must exist as an underlying tension in every teacher: the necessity to decide between the essentialist and contextualist mode of thought. And since this decision is so often not taken on an intellectual level, educational practices continue to suffer from theories based either on lopsidedness or opaqueness. A result of this is the common problem of a teacher not being able to take a clear stand as regards knowledge and interaction, as regards individual and society though it should not come as a surprise to learn that evolutionary learning processes could not be ascribed exclusively to society or individuals:

> Certainly the personality system bears the learning process of ontogenesis, and, to a certain extent, only individuals are capable of learning. However, social systems conform new structures by utilizing the learning capacities of their members in order to cope with problems that threaten system maintenance. In this respect the evolutionary learning process of societies is dependent on the competence of their individual members. These in turn acquire their competence, not as isolation monads, by the growing into the symbolic structure of their social world.[4]

The penetration of a pupil's lifeworld opens also the door for the misuse of education as an instrument to enforce thought, attitudes and behaviour. The meaningfulness of education could quickly disappear if its strategies are being perverted into propaganda instruments for political ideologies of totalitarian character. Fascism, communism, or a 'national culturalism' like 'Hindutva' would then turn out guidelines for instruction, and the balance of the personal and the social would tilt towards the mechanistically social at the expense of the emancipationally individual. In such a case, a brand of essentialist thinking would have taken over which were not counterpoised by analyses of contemporary political and educational reality; it would be openly in favour of those who have the means to manipulate political and educational ideas and with them reality. Over a short time they would have established new meanings in essentials by contextualizing them into their own mould, as for example in Nazi-Germany when 'justice' was wholly subjugated to Nazism, or in the Stalinist U.S.S.R. where it had to serve communism or in a communal India where it would possibly follow the tenets and ways of life of one religious spectre only.

Out of this we may deduce that truths are not necessarily established as attempts to correspond to the objective reality of a pupil's lifeworld but also, unscrupulously, as truths of a manipulated reality, whereby finally this manipulated reality may become part of an objective reality if enough time has elapsed and the manipulation is not anymore understood as manipulation but as—reality, that which exists and has 'always' existed so. (On the other hand we would have to question whether there is a reality which has never been manipulated?) These 'truths' are then used as alibis for something which has been created for a particular purpose. Reasoning would have to be transformed into a tool obeying political masters with the result of its degeneration into a dull formality of justifying preconceived rights and wrongs. That is why the pragmatic or humanistic conception of truth makes more sense in its insistence on the examination of practical, i.e., particular *consequences* of statements.[5]

Essentialism and the totality of a lifeworld have one thing in common and that is their mutual reinforcement. Being strictly confined to the 'purity' of each one of them would mean to have the other as a complementary. But this 'purity' does not exist, so that their relationship is one of constant feedback to the boundary occurrences of the two worlds. Essentialist thought surely offers justification to the totality of a lifeworld, whereas the latter functions as a mirror for essentialist thought.

Essentialism is a system of thought satisfied with the most general explanations of concepts. This will suit a person steeped in the totality of his lifeworld and seeing it as a fixture which should never be critically touched because the most general explanations are the most truthful but also the least threatening (and, by the way, the most philosophic ones). Agreement to lofty ideas is willingly given provided a commitment to a practical challenge is not included. A person in the totality of his lifeworld does prefer agreement to commitment for he feels more secure in his known totality than in the one which would be in a constant flux through the ruthless examination of values and judgments.

Teachers are no exception. Their professionalism in conveying ideas and ideals is, however, seldom matched by their behaviour in class where they like to advocate, for instance, 'justice' but often do not treat their pupils justly. If they were able to follow here a radical individuation in a Martin Buber like I-Thou relationship in which "(a)ll real living is meeting",[6] then they would not be afraid of losing their social roots and stability and with it may be a feeling for their lifeworld only to discover that their lifeworld really does exist and could be utilized for one's own benefit.

Martin Buber considers the "dialogical relation" as *the* educational relation which it characterized by the element of "inclusiveness" which is "the complete realization of the submissive person, the desired person, the 'partner', not by the fancy but by the actuality of the being". Inclusion is the opposite of "empathy" which means "the exclusion of one's own concreteness, the extinguishing of the actual situation of life, the absorption in pure aestheticism of the reality in which one participates"; instead inclusion

> is the extension of one's own concreteness, the fulfilment of the actual situation of life, the complete presence of the reality in which one participates. Its elements are, first, a relation of no matter what kind, between two persons, second, an event experienced by them in common, in which at least one of then actively participates, and, third, the fact that this one person, without forfeiting anything of the felt reality of his activity, at the same time lives through the common event from the standpoint of the other.[7]

Striving for this dialogical relation would make teachers and pupils aware of the fact that their lifeworlds would never shrink but expand, that they would enrich each other in knowledge and understanding. But, alas, practically too many teachers fear that they would lose a grip on themselves and the pedagogical situation if they entered into such a relation. Since they want to be unquestioned masters of themselves and their pupils and any pedagogical situation, they are ready to adopt essentialism as the smallest price to pay. With it they satisfy themselves by paying lip-service which sounds good rhetorically and demands nothing else. Not at all does it prevent what Buber calls "to 'transpose' oneself over there and in there" (there being any object)[8]. This transposition comes even more handy when teachers want to please people in political power. To adjust to *their* essentials means to help them keep their power, when it comes to problems like status, rights, salary, and evaluation. This kind of essentialism contributes at best to a political status quo which is a promising ground for complicity with those in political and economic power; and the guild of teachers have a known history of complicity with powers to be. Wherever dictatorships were established, teachers as a group were not known to be in the forefront of having raised their voices in protest and disgust.

But there is more to it. Teachers are also aware that in their pedagogical wish and desire to help others, the will to dominate is hidden, a psycho-social factor well known to those in the profession of help. It is interesting to note that this factor seems stronger in those teachers who claim to be "child-centred' and 'progressive' than those who, in a traditional sense, treat knowledge as the most important thing in educational encounters. Though I do refrain here from psychological interpretations, I do, however, see 'traditional' teachers no less vulnerable to the syndrome of individual power. Though they focus on knowledge as a seemingly neutral area in education, their relation to power is usually no less pronounced. There are two reasons for this. The first is that they tend to affirm a natural hierarchy between those who teach and those who learn. The teacher is the mature, and the learner is the less mature. This leads directly to the second reason: because he considers himself more mature, the teacher feels that he has the right to select knowledge—and he selects the knowledge he finds plausible for explaining a certain cause and the knowledge he knows. For him it would be a contradiction to select knowledge which may be implausible for the explanation of a fact, event or value, more so if he did not 'know' this knowledge. Politically and socially, these two types of teachers—the child-centred and the traditional—may be poles apart, their patronising behaviour in class seems to be the same though. Both would probably willingly subscribe to the observation that a curriculum is a "disciplining technology that directs how the individual is to act, feel, talk and 'see' the world and the 'self'", and that as such a "curriculum is a form of social regulation".[9]

Essentialism is important for the (educational) lifeworld when it comes to the question whether knowledge for a teacher and his pupils is generally true in the sense of 'reliable'. How does a teacher convince his pupils that his knowledge is reliable? And how does a pupil know whether his teacher's knowledge is generally true? There are no clear-cut answers to these questions, but to know about this problem—namely that there is a problem with truth in taught knowledge—makes a difference to a teacher's motivation for his own intellectual progress and to his readiness to accept it into his lifeworld and thus to enrich its totality from this epistemological angle. That is why he may be prepared to accept that new forms of knowledge, ultimately,

> grow out of conditions of collective life and do not depend for their emergence upon the prior demonstration by a theory of knowledge that they are possible; they do not, therefore, need to be first legitimized by an epistemology. The relationship is actually quite the reverse: the development of theories of scientific knowledge takes place in the preoccupation with empirical data and the fortunes of the former vary with those of the latter. The revolutions in methodology and epistemology are always sequels and repurcussions of the revolutions in the immediate empirical procedures for getting knowledge. Only through constant recourse to the procedure of the special empirical sciences can the epistemological foundations be made sufficiently flexible and extended so that they will not only sanction the claims of the older forms of knowledge (their original purpose) but will also support the newer forms. This peculiar situation is characteristic of all theoretical, philosophic disciplines.[10]

Teachers are more trustworthy in knowledge transmission when they can demonstrate to their pupils that they continuously acquire new knowledge and that they take scientific knowledge as a reference for other theories they like pupils to grasp and to contemplate upon. This is also an admission that there is only one certainty in the pedagogic endeavour of knowledge acquisition and transmission, viz. that it has to be an ongoing search and process. But it is also an expression of strength because it shows that the difference between teachers and learners need not be as wide as usually thought.

The gulf between teacher and pupil is, as a matter of fact, rather narrow. Note that it is logically easy to explain that 1 + 1 = 2 and, hence, does come close to the end of a learning process with the teacher having done his job and ready to proceed to the next item so far unknown to the pupil. But socially it opens the door to further operations and applications in which teacher and pupil can work closer together.

Each new problem solved by teachers *and* pupils together makes them see another one which has to be tackled afresh. In this sense knowledge provision is relational though knowledge is non-relational. Once the Pandora's box of questioning has been opened, there is only one way to deal with it: not to close it and not to give in to the pressures and temptations to declare it unknown, unknowable, or not desirable to be known. The principal task of teachers is just to keep this fire of questioning burning. It is, of course, not a panacea for convincing pupils to accept a teacher's knowledge as reliable, but it is an honest attempt and has a fair chance of succeeding because it shows the pupil that he is not the only one who is compelled to search. A precondition is that a teacher has learned to pursue knowledge for its own sake and not just for the fulfilment of a job at hand, say, to teach an item of a syllabus, knowing fully well that there is never an end in sight as long as the two, teacher and pupil, are involved in an educational relation. There is no retirement from the pursuit of knowledge. And "(s)ince there is always infinitely more to know, humility is always appropriate even when one knows what one does", viz. to try to know "that portion of the truth which is moving through one's mind at that moment."[11]

It is obvious that the constant pursuit of knowledge is strictly not only about truth and reliability but also about longing for clarity, and we must not believe that an automatic transformation of this pursuit into truth is possible. It is logically impossible because it would end in endless deductions which finally lead to axioms, unprovable or self-referential truths; but it is socially desirable as a trust-building method. And that is probably all that teachers can do: to clarify for the time being and to reproduce knowledge by pursuing it relentlessly to make pupils feel more certain about its reliability. Since teachers hardly, if ever, create new knowledge, the matter of truth is, therefore, for them, more of a social than of an epistemological order. A pupil, though he may be able to construct, mostly learns to trust teachers who have reconstructed knowledge for him and do place this knowledge intelligently before him. His mental faculties are mainly used to understand and not, or only occasionally, to create.

On the other hand, we have to consider that the difference between understanding and creation is a matter of degree. How far is creation the creation of something completely new and how often is it the creation of something relatively new? A pupil might well appreciate his understanding of something as a creation because it was not known to him before and he feels he is the only and first one to have understood it fully; at the same time this something is something of a routine piece of knowledge for the teacher. That means that in the provision of knowledge we should not easily work with absolutes; instead, we should feel encouraged to pursue an ongoing search for *the*-thing or the *no*-thing in the non-absolute world of education.[12]

We must, however, not be too concerned about this state because it is perfectly normal in education, has never been different, and probably will never be different, for education is always *re*construction and *re*discovery of knowledge (whereas science can contribute to the construction and discovery of knowledge). But there is a danger in this smug acceptance of normalcy, and this has also always been a danger in education: its inherent conservatism notwithstanding some bold attempts by people like Illich, Freire and Neill[13] to put education on a radical footing of liberal and conscientious approaches. Their experiments only confirm the deeply social character of knowledge and education.

This social character of knowledge and education cannot be wished away, it is there to stay because knowledge and education are always about relationships amongst the three actors of education—teacher, pupil and the curriculum. And it heads education for a compromise when it comes to the treatment of the individuation of knowledge.[14] Though they were perhaps more successful in socio-political liberation and child-centredness than others, these and other reformers are not different in their treatment of knowledge. The knowledge they want to see to be reproduced is also already out there; it is also already known to the teacher or facilitator beforehand, though he may pretend that this is not the case. He, however, invites pupils to rediscover it differently, in general by involving them much more in the process of learning, and by making it known to them that their participation counts in the reconstruction of knowledge. He gives them a feeling that it is as much their knowledge as it is his. Thus, his efforts are mainly methodological. But these reformatory approaches are equally conservative when it comes to the socio-epistemological because they restrict pupils also in what they can know and how, either to pass an examination, or to become a good person, or to lead a good life. Despite this their approaches can certainly help revolutionize education by preventing ruling and established classes from dominating it. Let us call this positive interference *social epistemology.*

To put it succinctly, social epistemology is the use of knowledge to create favourable conditions for justice and equality in a classroom, carrying the hope that these conditions may be later transferred to other areas of life like families and workplaces. There is an educational energy which grows from the commitment of social epistemology. The factors which generate this energy are the existing values and knowledge both impregnated with conflicting trends. They force us to take a stand, to judge between right and wrong, true and false, good and evil. Much of an educational practice revolves around these judgments and decisions and the conclusions drawn from them. A conscious social epistemology may be the only non-violent way of preventing teachers from exercising perpetual power in education. Social epistemology may also be successful in reducing power outside the field of education by enlightening about socio-cultural hegemonization and socio-political authoritarianism. This is, of course, a much more socially and politically active role of social epistemology than is normally understood by the concept. It is not only research and clarification[15], but it is perception, reflection and a call for action which culminates in "praxis", the authentic union of action and reflection.[16]

Hannah Arendt has pointed out the "potential" character of power—"(p)ower is always...a power potential and not an unchangeable, measurable and reliable entity like force or strength." Since all potentialities "can only be actualized but never fully materialized, power is to an astonishing degree independent of material forces, either of number or means".[17] That is why a single teacher can easily rule indefinitely over large classes, or a small management group can direct fairly large institutions. Education is always based on plurality of numbers and thus always entails a potentiality of power. That is why it has inescapably to do with power relationships. The postmodern conception of education in which the horizon of meaning has disappeared and the possibility of rationalizing the educational aspects of our existence has been rejected, would conceive power differently,

> not as something that one has or can use, but as something one is placed in the midst of. Bereft of what is valuable, the subject can only 'play' and follow the rules according to whoever is winning. Education is socialization in the direction of the greater benefit. It is nihilistic because nothing seems to be of value any longer. For some it will keep the power to change society in the direction of 'pleasure for the greater number', but it will no longer initiate into what is worthwhile, as nothing of that kind is left. The project of education vanishes in the nihilism of a degenerated aesthetics of everyday life.[18]

Social epistemology conceived as 'praxis' should be accepted to assume the role of a provider of a pedagogy of the values of modernity by combining the independent pursuit of knowledge selection and acquisition with the enlightening analysis of power relations. Both these activities will largely depend on the proper actualization of essentialist and contextualist pedagogical thought.

Essentialism as a force of totality and conservatism and contextualism as a force of fragmentation and liberalism are mutually dependent on each other. Any theory starts with knowledge. Knowledge is not at the end of a theory only, so to speak as its results, but already at its beginning thereby giving shape to a way to espouse a theory. A combination of thinking and using language within the former, without which a theory could not be formulated, is to reinforce theory building. It starts with available facts and beliefs and cannot be built without them since it cannot be built on nothing. Facts or beliefs as essentials are insofar contributing to a theory as they contain whole structures of meaning (which is a theory) of a concept.

Essentialist modes of thought claim now to have a higher level of theoretical thinking and explanation than contextualist modes. And since the totality of a person's lifeworld in all its numerous contexts is far too complex for even the most precise and detailed analysis to cover, leave alone to understand in full, the directive force of essentialism is supposed to lend a helping hand to order.

Intellectual order is to structure diffuse conditions and unclear explanations; it is further sought to clarify meanings in the mesh of ideas, norms and values found in any totality of a person and society. This can only be achieved by theory. Here essentialism assumes the progressive role of an arbiter who finally takes side in matters of confusion. Such an essentialism is surely another essentialism than the one which we, above, saw as a seducer into ordinary epistemologies held by teachers. While understood as a 'convenient word' with an essentialist flair and touch, it is a seducer, but challenged as a concept which gives theoretical order, it poses a genuine counterforce to an anything-goes contextualism. If this reminds us a bit of philosophy being the superior argumentation of merely empirical content as the highest form of knowledge and the most comprehensive of all the branches of knowledge, so be it. A suitable way of seeing it would be to understand essentialism as philosophy in social context, in the words of A. Banerjee, "as a self-critical expression of *lived* life".[19]

Another reason why contextualism is in need of essentialism is found in the force of practice to create its ideals without recourse to much elaboration. It is the lifeworld that continually provides material for the creation of visions and Great Ideas. If this material is taken at face value without reflection and refinement, ideals and Great Ideas seem to many to come directly from practical constraints and gain therefore in plausibility and need no further justification.

In daily educational practices we are often confronted with a situation which seems to sanction the precedence of the ideal of practice over the ideal of theory. We like to argue that what works in a classroom is right, and because it is attainable, it is also desirable. We are pragmatically interested in education as a type of activity for the purpose of a decent life. We are sure that the inexactitude of our aims need not be bound by reflected context. Latest since Wittgenstein do we know that meaning can be and should be use[21]—but even a non-used essential conveys also the meaning of a use. There is no non-use of something which exists, even if it exists only mentally. If we refrain from using it, we are also using it and are conveying with this non-use a certain meaning. If we know that 'justice' exists (in our mind or as an agreement in a society) and decide not to use it, then this is indeed not essentialism but something like symbolism in which a sign is looked on as presenting something. Only the decision to use a word makes it into an essential and a representation of essentialism.

To borrow a Russelian term, the "compresence"[21] of the existence of an essential and a contextual world will form a complex out of which we can take our direction towards the ideals of practice and theory. Many things can happen within a short span of time in our mind—so we can assume, also the formation of essentials and contextuals (to which we come presently in our next section). If we need contextualism to combat the authoritarian streak in essentialism, we also need essentialism to check the brutal rule of fact over imagination.

References

1. This is how Anthony Giddens characterizes Habermas's conception of "lifeworld" in "Reason Without Revolution? Habermas's *Theorlie des kommunikativen Handelns*", in Richard J. Bernstein (ed.), 1985, p. 101.
2. Jurgen Habermas, 1977, p. 209.
3. It is interesting to note that thinkers on education do prefer concepts like wholeness or completeness to lifeworld. See, for example, Paul Standish's five types of completeness in education (1995, p. 122): (1) "completeness is understood in terms of the initiation into public forms of knowledge and ways of understanding. The end of such

education is the educated man". (2) "completeness takes the form of an integrity realized where we are rational self-legislators, the autonomous architects of our own lives." (3) "completeness is to be achieved through the acquisition of a package of skills or competences." (4) "completeness involves the unfolding of an essential self. Sometimes it is through discovery, sometimes through something like the natural growth of a plant." (5) "rapidly developing in post-compulsory education, completeness is achieved through self-exploration. Through sharing or experience and through counselling we can achieve the wholeness of self-fulfilment a realization of our human potential." A reason for this preference may be found in the inherently idealistic thinking of probably any teacher for which wholeness or completeness based on constructing experience make sense as an overriding aim. That this would lead to relativism has been recently argued by Mark Olssen (1996) because the core epistemological proposition is "1. knowledge is actively constructed by the cognizing subject, not passively received from the environment; 2. coming to know is an adaptive process that organizes one's experiential world; it does not discover an independent, pre-existing world outside the mind of the knower." (p. 276) Following this radically, the teacher is seen as a 'provider of experiences' rather than a 'presenter of knowledge' (Ibid., p. 284). We should, however, also point out that one of the 20th century main thinkers on education, John Dewey, had a rather progressive understanding of totality which he named and saw as "context". Some references from his paper "Context and Thought" (1931) may illuminate his approach: "We grasp the meaning of what is said in our language not because appreciation of context is unnecessary but because context is so unescapably present. It is taken for granted." (John Dewey, 1960, p. 91) "Continued and systematic discourse enables us to determine the meaning of special symbols within the discourse only because it enables us to build up a nonverbal and non-symbolic context to which the whole refers." (Ibid., p. 91) "It is easy and too usual to convert abstraction from specific context into abstraction from all context whatsoever; another instance of the fallacy of unlimited extension." (Ibid., p. 104) Earlier he stated: "The fallacy of unlimited universalization is found when it is asserted, without...limiting conditions, that the goal of thinking, particularly of philosophic thought, is to bring all things whatsoever into a single coherent and all inclusive whole. Then the idea of unity which has value and import under specifiable conditions is employed with such unlimited extension that it loses its meaning." (Ibid., p. 95).

4. Jurgen Habermas, 1981, p. 269.
5. Though I disagree with the view that the pragmatic method should cover the notion "that the truth of any statement consists in the consequences, and particularly in their being *good* consequences" (William James, 1975, p. 230). I regard 'truth' as more of a dynamic concept that considers the way to truth as important as the product of truth. If one does so, the analysis of *bad* consequences would belong to the notion of truth as well. I suppose such an understanding of truth is a more educationally appropriate one.
6. Martin Buber, 1958, p. 11.
7. Martin Buber (1961, p. 97) in his address ("Rede über das Erzieherische") to the 3rd International Educational Conference at Heidelberg in 1925.
8. Ibid., p. 97.
9. Thomas S. Popkewitz, 1997, p. 132.
10. Karl Mannheim, 1982, p. 129.
11. Garry L. Baran, 1996, p. 252.
12. I have taken the term "no-thing" from P.J. Hiett, 1995, in which he argues that postmodernism "represents something very old", namely, "that one can't conjure absolutes out of a non-absolute world" (p. 197) and that postmodernism in "trying to express the inexpressable...sees this nothing as a negative no-thing, whereas the various liberatory techniques see it as a very positive thing. (p. 202)
13. Ivan Illich, 1977; Paulo Freire, 1970; A.S. Neill, 1982.
14. Here I do employ a much less technical-epistemological meaning of 'individuation' than, for example, Bertrand Russell (1992) who uses the principle of individuation to answer questions like "How shall we define the diversity which makes us count objects as two in a census?" or "What is meant by a 'particular'" (p. 310) Instead, I mean by individuation of knowledge the pedagogical practice to grant as much opportunity as possible to each pupil to go his own way in knowledge production, selection and acquisition.
15. As for example in Thomas S. Popkewitz, 1997, p. 132: "My use of *epistemology* is to *give reference* (emphasis mine) to how the systems of ideas in schooling organize perceptions, ways of responding to the world and conceptions of 'self'. The *social* in epistemology emphasizes the relational and social embeddedness of knowledge,

in contrast to (a)...philosophical concern with epistemology as a search for universal knowledge claims about the nature, origins and limits of knowledge."

16. Paulo Freire, 1977, p. 78.
17. Hannah Arendt, 1989, p. 200.
18. Paul Smeyers, 1995 (a), pp. 114-115; see also by the same author the second part of his paper (1995, b).
19. Archana Banerjee, 1989, p. 160. (emphasis mine).
20. Ludwig Wittgenstein's famous dictum that "the meaning of a word is its use in the language" was limited by him "(f)or a *large* class of cases—though not for all". (1973, 43).
21. Bertrand Russell, 1992, p. 315 ff.

5

Pedagogical Code-switching and Communicative Action

Education depends in its relationship between teacher and pupil upon expected agreement between the two. "In its minimal meaning it indicates that two subjects understand a linguistic expression in the same way; its maximal meaning is that between the two there exists an accord concerning the rightness of an utterance in relation to a mutually recognized normative background."[1] Without this expected agreement education would fail to be an activity which could possibly aim at a two-way communication.

The agreement is expected to be situated mainly in the realms of listening, believing and acknowledging. It is to listen to each other, to believe in each other's integrity and capability, and to acknowledge each other's specific role as mature or maturity-seeking persons. Listening to each other is to embrace the acceptance of the other's sincerity to say something meaningful, the teacher something which should make sense to the present or future life of the pupil, and the pupil something which demonstrates to the teacher that he, the pupil, is ready to understand. Over time this relationship of listeners can lead to a deeper relationship of the two, namely to believe in each other's openness in which the teacher is willing to believe in the pupil's desire to learn, and the pupil is willing to believe in the teacher's selection of the right knowledge and the proper methods to teach it. In a third step they may come to acknowledge each other's role as responsible people in education, the teacher seeing in his pupil a person who cannot but be a pupil, and the pupil to respect the teacher as someone who has the best in mind for his pupils.

Is this too ideal a description of the relationship between teacher and pupil which otherwise seems to be more characterized by indifference, mistrust and, occasionally, even hate? Yes and no. We have, unfortunately, to regard much in education as not being based on agreement but on force, dislike and opposition; many classrooms are battlegrounds of incompatibility and adversity. But we do find the ideal more often than we expect. This ideal is not so idealistic as it looks at first sight since much of the agreement in listening, believing and acknowledging is also the outcome of a good deal of compromising on either side, more so, however, by the pupil because he is qua role in a weaker position. Both teacher and pupil develop in the course of their relationship adjustment strategies for a decent pedagogical and social survival based on the presupposition that they have to be locked in an ethical relationship of some sort over time and might as well adjust.

The material condition of this ethics of relationship is found in the forms of power existing in *any* kind of education. Even the most child-centred kind of education contains strong elements of power execution, for example in the very decision by a teacher or another educational authority *to be* child-centred. This 'being' is *to grant* child-centredness, to give to others (the pupils) and to tolerate it (as teachers). Its power and force is already partly executed in the decision to select it as a strategy. Advancing *a* as a virtue and *b* as knowledge is to exercise power. Of course, there is a degree of intensity in the execution of power, but subtle or indirect power is also power. An educational hierarchy begs for it, the most progressive teacher's open attitude notwithstanding. So long as pupils have to agree to the presumably high morality of a teacher and the infallibility of his knowledge, so long is there an unequal relationship between the two which cannot be changed by any agreement. When a teacher has them all (morality and knowledge) and the pupil has not much of either, we cannot speak of both of them as being equal.

However, I maintain, agreement is nevertheless possible on a scale which can benefit the process of education and form it into a *more* open and equal one. Agreement has to be striven for since it is needed as perhaps the only way to, and source of, an education that is not engaged in indifference or hostility. The latter are too often at the base of a tense classroom climate. However imperfect, agreement is the sine qua non of education and should therefore not only depend on equality but also on the capacity to think rationally. Agreement based on the latter is the reason why so many pupils are able to go through the long span of (a mediocre) education without being damaged for life; and that is also the main reason why so many teachers are able to survive stressful classroom situations over a professional lifetime. If, however, a teacher claims his superiority only because of his status for an authority has bestowed on him some of its own authority, then the potential of agreement between him and his pupils will weaken. If, on the other hand, his morality and knowledge are objects of continuous reflection, then the potential of agreement can be kept at a high level despite adverse conditions like lack of resources or an out-of-date syllabus. Ordinary educational thought tends to weaken the potential of agreement whereas reflective educational thought is going to strengthen it.

At this stage, I should like to formulate the hypothesis that the *connection of essentialist and contextualist modes of thought* leads to a maximum exploitation of the rational potential of agreement between teacher and pupil. Let us unravel this in two stages: first, by asking 'what is this connection?' and second, 'how can it help raise the willingness to agree?' In brief, the answer to the first is *pedagogical code-switching*, and to the second, *communicative action*. The compresence of the two in virtually parallel actions protects teacher and pupil against an extreme essentialism and a crushing contextualism and becomes thus the foundation for the necessity to agree.

To the first question, 'what is the connection between essentials and contextuals as *the* representatives of essentialist and contextualist thought respectively?' This connection is to be found and traced in the *continuous process of transformation of essentials into contextuals and vice versa.* I hope to be able to demonstrate this with the help of an example of a growing curriculum-consciousness of teachers and pupils alike. The example is going to describe the transformation of 'non-violence' by using Frantz Fanon's ideas on decolonization in a teaching unit on the Algerian Revolution.

Non-violence as Essential and Contextual

In this unit, I attempted in class to show that essentialist and contextualist modes of pedagogical thought together can bring about a fulfilling educational experience for both pupil and teacher. It is an example taken from my work as a teacher of history and was a unit taught over four weeks meeting daily for one lesson. The class consisted of ten pupils (six girls and four boys) from grade 12.

As a 'fulfilling educational experience' I understand two things: first, to work with clear knowledge, to address the potentialities of all pupils, and to arouse their interest in the topic (hoping that these qualities would also be a fulfilling experience for them), and second, to work for a teaching learning process out of which gradually a curriculum-consciousness can emerge for both pupils and teacher. This is to be developed in a participatory manner in class on the one hand and internalized in an autobiographical aloneness on the other. Curriculum-consciousness is to be achieved when both pupils and teachers do regularly reflect on the nature of knowledge conveyed, on the purpose why this particular knowledge has been selected, and on the ways how it has been taught.

The topic of the unit "The Algerian Revolution (1954-1962)" was supposed to be taught mainly through essentialist and contextualist conceptualizations of the phenomena of 'violence' and 'non-violence'. These conceptualizations were to be gained in two ways, first, by using them as a pedagogic technique in the teaching and learning relationship (i.e., everyone was invited to reflect on his own violence and non-violence towards other class members, his family and friends, people in general), and second, by studying the violence-non-violence problem as a possibly central challenge to the people of Algeria in their fight against French colonialism. With this two-pronged strategy I hoped to come nearer to a realization of curriculum-consciousness.

The unit was divided into six parts out of which the third and fourth took up around half of the time available:

1. *Introduction:* To discuss the two aims of the unit (a fulfilling educational experience and curriculum-consciousness). To become familiarized with the concept of non-violence by reading excerpts from Vinoba, a disciple of Gandhi.
2. *The historical setting:* To convey knowledge about the causes of the Revolution, the Revolution itself and the

consequences of the Revolution through lectures by the teacher and through presentations of brief papers by the pupils.

3. *The idea of anti-colonialism:* To understand the growing self-awareness in the "Third World" against Western colonialism by reading parts of Frantz Fanon's *The Wretched of the Earth.*
4. *The idea of Algeria*: To study a typical liberation struggle, the forming of a nation, the self-definition of guerillas, and the creation of a new kind of society by reading parts of Frantz Fanon's *A Dying Colonialism.*
5. *Algeria today:* To focus on the time after 1992 and the growing conflict between the Algerian Government and the Islamic movement by using contemporary sources (newspapers, magazine, television).
6. *Evaluation:* (a) Test of historical knowledge. (b) Why was it a fulfilling educational experience and why was it not? (c) Discussion of curriculum-consciousness with an emphasis on the conceptualization of non-violence as an essential and a contextual.

What follows below is exemplary, a schematic account of a discussion process which took place in sections 3 and 4 and its assessment in section 6 (b) and (c) respectively. In section 3, the chapter *Concerning Violence* from Fanon's *The Wretched of the Earth* was read, whereas in section 4 the chapter *The Algerian Family* from his *A Dying Colonialism* was made the point of departure.

Both these chapters on the fight for liberation with respect to the grave traumata inflicted on the Algerian family and on the anti-colonial struggle as regards the use of violence respectively demonstrate, as the two books do in general, Fanon's analytical approach which has been recently treated as a "dramatic dialectical narrative" and not as one that accords "utterences in his texts unambiguous status of prepositional statements and doctrines."[2] This reading, shared by this author, provides a middle ground strategy between postmodern relativism and the search for a monolithic philosophy. Fanon's dramatic dialectical narrative is highly suitable for the demonstration of a transformation of essentials and contextuals. It makes it easier for pupils to follow arguments and to grasp the gradual process of transformation.

In the family-chapter, Fanon's conclusion is that

> (e)ach member of this family has gained in individuality what it has lost in its belonging to a world of more or less confused values. Individual persons have found themselves facing new choices, new decisions. The customary and highly structured patterns of behaviour that were the crystallization of traditional ideas suddenly proved ineffective and were abandoned.[3]

In the course of the war against the French "the people came to realize that if they wished to bring a new world to birth they would have to create a new Algerian society from top to bottom".[4] In the backdrop of a war-like and revolutionary violence, a social system had to be completely changed either violently or non-violently:

- In the relationship between son and father the "level of consciousness" was decisive, the father usually lagging far behind the son, the son becoming the "militant" and thus replacing the son and trying to indoctrinate the father. The father would respond by recognizing the new values "and to invoke other authorities", for example, by reminding the militant son of the principle of discipline within the revolutionary group.[5]
- An even more drastic change occurred in the relationship between daughter and father. A child-woman having to learn the "the higher value of the man" and to be married off at puberty, the daughter in the traditional family accepted this "as a liberation, as a deliverance, as finally achieving her balance". Her joining the revolution changed all this and led to another liberation. "The woman-for-marriage progressively disappeared, and gave way to the woman-for-action." And with this the father's attitude underwent a radical change as well, even towards those of his daughters who had not joined the revolutionary groups. He would not demand of her anymore to be silent, nor would he question her moral behaviour living with men in her group. The girl was "inviting her father to

undergo a kind of mutation, to wrench himself free of himself".[6]

- And so changed the relations between elder and younger brother and, probably more importantly, between wife and husband. A new openness was established between husband and wife during the revolutionary fight, and the "united militant couple...became the rule". In this process the couple became considerably more closely knit, and what could formerly be defined as mere cohabitation included during the revolution a multiplicity of points of communication. "The mingling of fighting experience with conjugal life deepens the relations between husband and wife and cements their union. There is simultaneous and effervescent emergence of the citizen, the patriot and the modern spouse".[7] In the wake of this, marriage often ceased to be an arrangement between families, and divorce was not anymore the easy prerogative of the husband.[8]

Transformations of essentialist concepts into contextualist and vice versa occur before, during and after an educational practice. But only for the sake of educational 'measurement' do we understand here educational practice as an action with a clear beginning and a clear end. In reality it cannot be split into time frames since learning is a continuous process of relating the former to the latter and the latter to the former. Teaching units are only an artificial means to organize pedagogical matter for a managerial and administrative purpose. But certainly there is also the normative pressure of an educational practice once it is organized by a teacher and to be followed by a pupil. Only in such an understanding of practice may we speak of a beginning and an end of the same. Let us now trace some transformations of non-violence in our example.

In the initial stage

From the essential 'non-violence' to the contextual 'non-violence'

We (here always meant as the class including the teacher) have a basic understanding of non-violence which has been significantly shaped by non-violence as a means to achieve the independence of India. For us it is love, fearlessness, cooperation, faith in constructive work, balance in thinking, equanimity of mind, seeking non-differences in differences, perpetual sacrifice, joy in sacrifice, bravery, a continuous action.[9] We have been told that it needs discipline and planning, that it is neither "lenient tolerance" nor "intolerable vigorous restraint", and that it can be achieved only through the "quest of spirit".[10] Ultimately, it should be "truth".[11] And we are also well-trained to accept a non-violent action as a political technique inseparable from belief systems which emphasize non-violence as a moral principle.[12]

But now we are *confused* having learned about the political and social success of the Algerian Revolution: the country became independent and the individual (father, son, daughter, husband and wife) developed new attitudes which certainly helped them lead a more modern life. They have helped shape future generations with their new outlook. But this was achieved by joining the violent fight against the French!

Fanon opens his chapter *Concerning Violence* with the statement that "decolonization is always a violent phenomenon" because it "is quite simply the replacing of a certain 'species' of men by another 'species' of men" and, thus, "a programme of complete disorder".[13] The intention of the decolonization process to place the last first and the first last "will only come to pass after a murderous and decisive struggle" between the French "settler" and the Algerian "native" and can only triumph if all means to turn the scale, "including, of course, that of violence" are being used[14]:

> The native who decides to put the programme (of decolonization, BP) into practice, and to become its moving force, is ready for violence at all times. From birth it is clear to him that this narrow world, strewn with prohibitions, can only be called in question by absolute violence.[15]

Fanon continues to argue that the "violence which has ruled over the ordering of the colonial world" has created a "mental picture of action" in the colonized people to destroy the colonial world, to bury it in the depth of the earth, and to expel it from the country.[16] The problem, for Fanon, is to lay hold of the violence of the colonized people which is too often expressed in myths and religion and canalized by the emotional outlets of dance and possession by spirits, and to change its direction.[17] National parties and bourgeois elites would not help much in this endeavour because they were only "violent in their words" but "reformist in their attitudes"; and their aim was to receive more power for themselves.[18] On the other hand, the native knows that justice cannot be bought in the colonial framework, so only the militant group could accomplish the "death of the settler"[19] and to respond to colonial violence with counter-violence. This violence

> binds them together as a whole, since each individual forms a violent link in the great chain, a part of the great organism of violence which has surged upwards in relation to the settler's violence in the beginning. The groups recognize each other and the future nation is already indivisible. The armed struggle mobilizes the people; that is to say, it throws them in one way and in one direction.[20]

Once so unified and mobilized, each man's consciousness would be introduced to "the ideas of a common cause, of a national destiny and of a collective history" and would thus help in the building-up of the nation.[21] In his final argument for violence, Fanon maintains that "violence is a cleansing force" which "frees the native from its inferiority complex and from his despair and inaction" and "makes him fearless and restores his self-respect".[22]

After the appropriation of Fanon's line of argumentation in class we had to ask ourselves: is then the way of non-violence as it is connected to Indian Independence the only way of seeing it? Was the conversion of the British not more humane than the destruction of the French? Could the Algerians have done the same as the Indians? Perhaps, but the Indian society with its numerous diversities hardly changed with the success of the freedom struggle, whereas the Algerian society did so radically, and in a very short time—admittedly it was less diversified. If violence is cleansing, then is non-violence non-cleansing? If violence works only for a just cause, does this mean that the Algerian fight against colonialism was not just? Non-violence is sometimes impossible, for example when confronted by a force like Nazism. "Gandhi's insistence on non-violence in the struggle against fascism was a counsel not so much of perfection as of pathos!"[23] And do we not know more instances where "force has been the midwife of new social forms emerging out of the old"[24] as in the case of the

Algerian family. One need not idolize violence—but could it be a complementary to non-violence?

We have, in class, now reached a point where a set piece of non-violence has been, with the help of further knowledge, deeply questioned. Provisional answers have made the pupils and the teacher more cautious in stating what they think non-violence is and can achieve. Confusion has helped in this transformation. It is not simply a matter of making up one's mind between here Vinoba/Gandhi and there Fanon; it was enough to establish this polarization to initiate change in conceptualization—an essential on its way to becoming a contextual.

In the middle stage

From the contextual 'non-violence' to the essential 'non-violence'

We have reached a stage where we are trying out both our options in thought-experiments and amongst ourselves. Quickly questions come up. When do we have in class situations which resemble British and French colonialism? When are the compulsions of circumstances so strong that we have to execute violence against each other? Non-violence is said to "express itself through the *ordinary activities of life*".[25] Then let us look at ourselves to find out when and why we are non-violent and when and why we are violent. When do we act alone, and when are we part of a group, maybe a gender group, in these ordinary activities? And how much does this group, maybe the boys in class, influence our violent or non-violent behaviour? Non-violence means to keep our promises. Only towards our families, our class, or also towards ourselves? Let us think of limiting or eventually destroying the power of a teacher. Here the deliberation in class took up Hannah Arendt's thesis that power and violence are opposites

> (w)here the one rules absolutely, the other is absent. Violence appears where power is in jeopardy, but left to its own course it ends in power's disappearance. This implies that it is not correct to think of the opposite of violence as non-violence; to speak of non-violent power is actually redundant. Violence can destroy power; it is utterly incapable of creating it. Hegel and Marx's great trust in the dialectical 'power of negation', by virtue of which opposites do not destroy but smoothly develop

> into each other because contradictions promote and do not paralyze development, rests on a much older philosophical prejudice: that evil is no more than a private modus of the good, that good can come out of evil; that, in short, evil is but a temporary manifestation of a still-hidden good.[26]

We have to learn that we have to study the nature and roots of power; but despite this we have come to accept the limitations of both the options, to limit or to destroy the power of the teacher. We have (still) great difficulties to decide. However, it is beginning to dawn on us that, whatever the situation, whether it is the Algerian people in the late 50s or us today in class, we have to be prepared to universalize *and* singularize our political and educational experience and to welcome this conceptual *tension* in non-violence. For this tension allows us again another essentializing, i.e., generalizing exercise since it guards us from searching for one-dimensional answers.

After the educational practice

From the essential 'non-violence' to the contextual 'non-violence'

We are still reluctant about the worthiness of our original essential and we have accepted that we have to (permanently?) redefine it. Every new *redefinition*, after passing through contextualizing experiences, turns out to be a new essential. And we also come back to know that using the concept of non-violence in a different situation will change our understanding and internalization of it. We can do this out of class by reflecting on our roles in our families and compare them to the Algerian experience of changing values and communication patterns among various family members. How have we assumed our roles in our families? Was it an integrative process of slow-paced adjustment which is then often taken for non-violence and identified as a constructive activity or was it in a myth-bursting eruption against family harmony which could be characterized also as a destructive activity? But also a liberatory—and suddenly we realize that we are back to the initial stage of the educational practice, or better to a *new* intitial stage, having gone through a variety of arguments on the political, social, educational and personal level. We know that we have made our life more complex and also richer in refinement, knowledge, thought, and experience.

If such a process is finally evaluated, nearly all the actors tend to confirm that it was a fulfilling educational experience because it tried to integrate knowledge with social life: how do we come to decisions, what shall we do with competition amongst ourselves, where are the boundaries of ethical values for us, when do we become masters of our own nature? were some of the existential problems discussed with the help of Fanon and the Algerian Revolution. Later we found that the factual knowledge we had to acquire was easy to assimilate and to retain. But we also reflected on the appropriateness of the example for the purpose of learning about a specific anti-colonial struggle, about colonialism in general, about colonialism in relation to violence and non-violence, about a specific social system (the Algerian family before and after the Revolution), and about the moral questions involved in political and social change. We have become more conscious about our curriculum, i.e., about that which we have to learn (and to teach), why and how. The example itself was questioned by some as an ill-selected one while others found it appropriate and stimulating. Alternative examples were found and suggested. To involve the curriculum question into the educational practice has invited us to reflect on the means and ends of our education.

The whole transformative process as regards non-violence did not occur in a sudden flash and on the spur of the moment. Education seldom results in a new perception all of a sudden; it usually creates them over time for which a dialogue, a discourse is needed. Though I do not rule out that immediate perceptions of transformations are possible in some cases. But since we expect education to be a planned activity in which perceptions are moulded and gained slowly, a discourse seems to be an appropriate method to prepare transformations of the kind described above. *Confusion, tension, redefinition* are some of the characteristics and results of a discourse which can finally produce agreement between people and/or within oneself.

Transformations from an essentialist concept to a contextualist one, and vice versa, as the example has shown, are perpetual redefinitions. They are not learned in doing radically new things because there is always the background of knowledge we already possess and with which we have to operate whether we do this consciously or not. We cannot free ourselves from prior knowledge and make it undone. We have, for instance, conceptions of non-violence long before reading Gandhi and Fanon. These conceptions have been formed in private experiences with parents, teachers and friends, or in public experiences based on reports of others in politics, economics or sociology. I do not see here 'redefinition' as the major problem or pedagogical hurdle; it is the 'perpetual' which demands an always alert teacher or pupil who in one moment thinks he is on safe ground only to find himself thrown into new knowledge which, by the sheer weight of its quality and quantity, demands of him a perpetual readiness to transform even the most intimate beliefs. What can make us do so? What can be the meeting ground for this play with losing and gaining knowledge?

Gaining and losing knowledge takes place in a communicative action on the meeting ground of a Grand Morality and the Fragments of an educational environment. We are pushed, on the one hand, by our traditions, values and norms to obey our Morality only to see, on the other, difficulties and differences increase. Gaining and losing in such a trap-like situation occurs in the realms of relevance, validity and clarity.

Our Grand Morality, though of universal character and claim, is always historical. Whether in a religious or non-religious mode, it is always handed down from a past to a present. To have a Grand Morality is to have a past. Only in times of great upheaval could we directly witness a Grand Morality being formed—however, even this is often only a change of an existing ethics keeping a lot of the earlier intact. While a Grand Morality remains rather unmoved, our (educational) environment undergoes rapid changes and becomes fragmented; and more and more situations take over forming of what is relevant and valid. It is immensely difficult to get clear about things.

Non-violence continues to mean a lot to us—but why shall it bother us when we are not directly involved or affected by a situation which is or is not in need of it? We do live only in one Fragment—and non-violence may be important in another. In not *contextualizing* non-violence it remains an empty shell in the form of a past essential; and in not *essentializing* it further, the context out of which it has sprung would remain isolated and not examined with the help of Great Ideas. In either case, inaction on our part is the cause. Contextualizing an idea cannot be done without chipping from an ideal of non-violence, i.e., losing or discarding some of its earlier content, though it also gains in dimensions by adding new facets and dilemmas. In turn, essentializing a practice is not possible without aiming at a consensus of the idea(l) and the practice, i.e., the utopian potential is regressing.

All this happened in our example of the teaching unit on the Algerian Revolution where the Great Ideas of freedom met with the other Great Idea of non-violence in conditions which demanded of the Algerian people at that time and the pupil who studies these conditions in class today to select amongst choices in an intricate network of historical-cum-contemporary and personal-cum-social situations. Essentializing and contextualizing were deeply interwoven processes in our example which forced teacher and pupils to leave the grounds of neutrality more than once. The phase of Algerian history studied by the class has initiated us into a rather stringent introspection of our own values and attitudes. I dare say that such a teaching-learning approach embodies, besides clear, factual knowledge, the normative content of the Enlightenment which was expressed in the ideas of self-consciousness, self-determination and self-actualization[27] accepting the view that the self is a creation of society.

I do not maintain that teachers and pupils are involved in this process of transformation with always a vision and purpose, but I would not argue either that the whole process is only an instinctive one. In a classroom, claims of relevance, validity and clarity have their due share in steering this process in a rather systematic order. This order may be favoured by a clear understanding of Habermas's communicative action which could be used as the foundation of pedagogical code-switching.

According to Habermas, a communicative action occurs "whenever the actions of the agents involved are coordinated not through egocentric calculations of success, but through acts of reaching understanding."[28] This understanding is to be supported by consensual speech actions which are based on a presupposition that participants know "what mutual recognition of reciprocally raised validity claims means" and how to rely "on a shared definition of the situation and thereupon act consensually". This communication can also occur "on the basis of a symbolically established intersubjective relationship...even if (one) is actually alone with a book, a document, or a work of art."[29] Habermas gives four conditions for such a discourse[30]:

1. each subject who is capable of speech and action is allowed to participate in discourses.
2. (a) each is allowed to call into question any proposal.
   (b) each is allowed to introduce any proposal into the discourse.
   (c) each is allowed to express his attitudes, wishes and needs.
3. no speaker ought to be hindered by compulsion—whether arising from inside the discourse or outside of it— from making use of the rights secured under (1) and (22).[31]

These rules are recommended for procedures in class; they virtually guarantee a communicative basis for an equal participation of pupils and teacher and, in their next step, are a presupposition for a consensus theory of truth which ought to be regarded as a condition for a permanent process of essentializing and contextualizing, i.e., pedagogical code-switching.[32]

Central, for Habermas, to a communicative action and an agreement of the listener with the speaker is to meet the validity claims of a speech act. The essential speech acts, to which we are subject when we are engaged in a communicative action, consist of making four validity claims: intelligibility, truth, correctness, and sincerity:

> The successful performance of a speech-act essentially requires that in issuing an utterance, the speaker implicitly claims that what is said is *intelligible*, that the propositional content is *true*, that the performative part is *correct* or legitimate, and that what is believed is expressed with *sincerity*. The hearer, in the same way, understands the utterance by generally assuming that the speaker is sincere, that he takes what is said to be true and so on.[33]

Habermas holds that the establishment of a relation in which at least two persons come to an understanding about something is the result of a successful speech act.[34]

In an important innovation Habermas qualifies the traditional centrality of truth

> by distinguishing between three 'validity-claims', which he categorizes as 'truth' (Wahrheit), 'rightness' (Richtigkeit) and 'truthfulness' (Wahrhaftigkeit). The first of these three terms describes the cognitive status of claims about the objective world, the second the normative status of the rules governing interpersonal relations within the social world, and the last the expressive status of claims concerning the subjective experiences of the individual.[35]

This distinctively modern characteristic to distinguish between the cognitive, normative and affective gives rise to a "discourse theory of truth" governed by the idea that consensus is the immanent telos of language. For Habermas

> it is part of the pragmatic meaning of making an assertion that the speaker commits him- or herself to the provision of grounds for what has been asserted, should the validity of the truth-claim raised be questioned. Such a process of questioning and resolving the validity of disputed claims takes place through the form of argumentation, relieved from the immediate pressure of action, which Habermas terms 'discourse' (Diakurs). According to this conception, speakers of a language necessarily presuppose that it is possible to resolve, and possess an intuitive knowledge of how to resolve consensually, disputed validity claims, since otherwise language would be unable to fulfil what Habermas takes to be its central function of co-ordinating action through agreement.[36]

In sum, a communicative action would result in "sensibleness" which, according to Habermas, is the convergence of truth, truthfulness and appropriateness or rightness.[37]

Teachers and pupils who can realize that they are part of a transformative process through their reflection-in and reflection-on the same attribute to their education, the liberatory and emancipatory means *the* word as truth. To become aware of oneself as a part of education through language is then the essentialist aim of education, and to become conscious of the knowledge and the curriculum placed before us is then the contextualized aim. Both may be operating at times with the same word, but their use and meaning would shift in new situations and challenges.

Emancipation of teachers and pupils is characterized by their permenent reflection on, and participation in, communicative actions safeguarded, once entertained, by language in an intersubjectivity of unconstrained agreement and "relieved from the immediate pressure of action".

But despite the construing of ideal speech situations and the willingness to agree, it is questionable whether to have a 'pure' communication is possible. Too much of everyday communication in a classroom is *not ideal* but overtly strategic and covertly manipulative. Not all teaching is, or can be, discursive.[38] That is why we are often left with the problem of how to deal with compromise which even a universal pragmatics that analyses general conditions for communicative actions[39] cannot fully overcome. We could claim that compromise is being easily practised in education through the fundamental proposal that agreement is the immanent telos of language, but there is a fine line between agreement and compromise which has something to do with the different stands towards power. Both appeal to a pragmatic attitude by taking conditions into account, and both are attached to the force of finding a solution to a problem, but both are different reactions to power reality as well.

Communicative action can be crushed under the weight of power relations which are wholly losided in favour of the teacher despite teacher and pupil using language all the time. Compromise can deal with these unequal power relations by simply not resisting long enough to arrive at truth, truthfulness and rightness. It leads to complacency and status quo thinking. It does not support political counter-forces which would aim at structural changes in the hierarchy of educational institutions and their societal environment. These counterforces could be found, for example, in such strategies as suggested by Ivan Illich ("disestablishing") and Erich Fromm ("disobedience").

In his well-known works of the 70s, Illich criticized the consumption of teaching and learning as a performance equal to the consumption of any other goods—the subject has become a commodity, and the institution school a warehouse. He pleaded for a new direction in content by always keeping in mind to what use it can be put. His belief in a "global schoolhouse" appears naive today in a world of technology with virtually no rules and conditions attached and thereby open to a fierce educational capitalism. But his idea of a "free school" by first disestablishing the old, non-free school could still be an ideal any teacher would like to work for:

> Free schools, to be truly free, must meet two conditions: first, they must be run in such a way as to prevent the reintroduction of the hidden curriculum of graded attendance and certified students studying at the feet of certified teachers. And more important, they must provide a framework in which all participants, staff and pupils, can free themselves from the hidden assumptions of a schooled society.[40]

Such a free school could practise what Fromm calls "disobedience"; it is *the* virtue of a humanist radicalism which should question every institution and every idea from the standpoint whether it hinders or helps man's capacity of greater joy and aliveness. Disobedience

> is an act of the affirmation of reason and will. It is not primarily an attitude directed *against* something, but *for* something: for man's capacity to see, to say what he sees, and to refuse to say what he does not see. To do so he does not need to be aggressive or rebellious; he needs to have his eyes open, to be fully awake, and willing to take the responsibility to open the eyes of those who are in danger of perishing because they are half asleep.[41]

Disestablishing educational structures and disobeying complacent attitudes would be direct forces to oppose the present form of schooling and the powers behind it. They would certainly depend on material conditions for dialogue and discourse. Probably the most important material condition to be created would be an atmosphere where disestablishment and disobedience were allowed and promoted.

In such a scenario, Habermas could now argue that disobeying and disestablishing are surely only to be achieved through language in a communicative action. I would agree that this is a precondition but would insist on additional measures so that one would *not* be relieved from the pressure to take action. These measures would have to have an immediate effect on power relations in a classroom and through them gradually on the whole educational system. Amongst them would be to make attendance for pupils voluntary, to allow pupils to select their own teachers, to permit pupils to walk out of education without facing sanctions, to introduce new forms of assessment, and so forth. For teachers it could mean to work for a kind of status to be 'self-employed' within a 'pedagogical federation' which would give them a chance to accept only as many pupils as they want and can handle properly, to teach only what they know well and not to just fill in, and so forth.

If we ever want to see an education realized in consonance with modern child psychology, which is the minimum any public should demand, we have to arrange classrooms where the fullest liberty of thought is possible, where the "child's immediate milieu must serve as a resource for the rediscovery of accepted knowledge", where children "must have the freedom to create their own models of knowledge and about the world", where learning "must provide for opportunities for children to be physically active", and where classroom activities "must resonate and extend the child's life at home and in its surroundings".[42]

To build up an atmosphere and consciousness in which these conditions could be introduced and flourish would mean to create an environment that fosters, on a Habermasian basis, code-switching in communicative actions to allow essential and contextual concepts to be tried out and formed in a free interplay. But it also needs the environment of something like a free school where disestablishing hidden agendas and disobeying as a positive attitude of responsibility would be steadily nurtured to reinforce themselves finally as structural changes. An education based on modern child psychology could only be practised successfully in institutions which are prepared to generate critical discourses among *all* of their members.

References

1. Jürgen Habermas, 1979, p. 3.
2. Ato Sety-Otu, 1996, p. 3.
3. Frantz Fanon, 1970 p. 81.
4. *Ibid.*, p. 85.
5 *Ibid.*, pp. 84-87.
6. *Ibid.* pp. 87-91.
7. *Ibid.*, pp. 92-96.
8. *Ibid* ., pp. 96-98.
9. Vinoba, 1981, pp. 53-54.
10. *Ibid.*, p. 58.
11. *Ibid.*, p. 55.
12. See to this Gene Sharp, 1987.
13. Frantz Fanon, 1977, p. 27.
14. *Ibid.*, p. 28.
15. *Ibid.*, p. 29.
16. *Ibid.*, p. 31.
17. *Ibid.*, p. 45.
18. *Ibid.*, p. 46.
19. *Ibid.*, p. 67.
20. *Ibid.*, p. 73.
21. *Ibid.*, p. 73.
22. *Ibid.*, p. 74.
23. Hiren Mukerjee, [4]1991, p. 213.
24. *Ibid.*, p. 211.
25. Mohit Chakrabarti, 1987, p. 540.
26. Hannah Arendt, 1970, p. 56.
27. Jürgen Habermas in his paper "The New Intimacy between Politics and Culture: Theses on Enlightenment in Germany", in Jürgen Habermas, 1989, p. 203.
28. Jürgen Habermas, 1984, pp. 285-286.
29. Jürgen Habermas, 1979, p. 9.

30. This is how Habermas comments on the two forms of communication: "Under the heading 'action' I introduce the area of communication in which we silently presuppose and recognize implied validity claims in engagements (even in assertions) in order to exchange information (that is, behaviour-related experiences). Under the heading 'discourse' I introduced the form of communication characterized by argumentation in which validity claims that have become problematic are made the subject of discussion and examined relative to their legitimacy. In order to entertain a discourse, we must in a way step out of behavioural and experiential contexts; here we exchange not information, but rather arguments that serve to establish (or reject) validity claims." Quoted from *Vorstudien und Ergänzungenzur Theoric de, kommunikativen Handelns* (1984, pp. 130-131), in Detlef Horster/Willem van Reijen, 1992, p. 31.

31. Quoted from *Moralbewustsein und kommunikatives Handeln* (1983, p. 99), in S.K. White, 1988, p. 90.

32. Not only for a classroom routine are these rules significant, but also for a wider educational policy as Nigel Blake (1992, p. 46) has pointed out: "...it is the rules of discourse which ground the educational principles I wish to defend for a pluralist society. Rule 1, that anyone may participate in discourses, surely implies that all cultures have a right to a voice in the curriculum. Rule 2 (a) to 2 (c) entail that all such cultures must be equally open to critique—any proposition may be entertained or questioned, and the needs and wishes of individuals are relevant to critique—including the critique of a culture by those who live within it. Thus these educational principles are...constitutively modern, since they follow from rules of discourse which are constitutively modern."

33. Arundhati Mukherji, 1997, p. 33.

34. *Ibid.*, p. 33.

35. Peter Dews, 1995, p. 266.

36. *Ibid.*, pp. 264-265.

37. Detlef Horster, 1989, p. 306.

38. See to this Nigel Blake, 1995, who asserts "that discourse is essential *as an element* in the curriculum" but that even if "teaching is properly discursive, it still need not conform to the conditions of the ideal speech situation". (p. 361)

39. See to this Detlef Horster/Willem van Reijen, 1992, pp. 24-31, and Arundhati Mukherji, 1997.

40. Ivan Illich, 1980, p. 87. See also his chapter "Why We Must Disestablish Schools" in Ivan Illich, 1977, pp. 9-31.
41. Erich Fromm, 1984, p. 33.
42. Krishna Kumar, 1995, p. 15. Kumar sees in these demands a striking similarity to Gandhi's vision with modern child psychology in order to reform the system of education. Even if we add to this another Gandhian feature, namely, to bridge the school with the world of work by introducing (traditional) handicraft training as a crucial activity around which the whole curriculum should revolve, we must not overlook the lack of theory in Gandhi's educational ideas as well as in those of modern child psychology. They are both too much involved with well-being (less though in Gandhi's case) and giving an activity orientation to the curriculum. This makes them evade deeper questions of knowledge, concept formulation and reflective educational thought.

6

The Circle of Educational Modernity

I have attempted to show that essentialism and contextualism represent two systems of thought which constitute educational epistemologies and that their corresponding modes of pedagogical thought are in turn the foundations of educational practices: Essentialist and contextualist concepts are used within them as operating categories and function, thus, as directive principles for theory and practice. Though mutually dependent on each other, teachers tend to follow one of the two more than the other.

In an essentialist pedagogy, teachers select general content, so to speak the idea behind a number of connected facts, and try to teach a knowledge which is traditional, well received, well-known, and a definite part of a canon. They feel secure in this because this knowledge is considered to be certain since it is based on either 'history' or 'shared science'. In a contextualist pedagogy, teachers select specific content, so to speak the many facts of an idea, and try to teach empirical knowledge which is regarded as a less certain form of knowledge. This would include thinking and learning about alternatives in knowledge as well as in the socio-political framework of education.

Conscious of this dichotomy, a teacher ought to initiate interactions which would result in a balance of the two modes of thought. A teacher in the essentialist mode would have to convince himself of how important it is to think contextually and how much he needs to think about 'application'; whereas a teacher in the contextualist mode would have to accept the need for 'abstraction'. The instrument to bring about this shift is an action guided by communicative reason leading to a consensus/discourse theory of truth.

In this process, it is not only the pupil who is asked to develop reflective consciousness, but also the teacher who has to nurture critical reflection as a procedural value because there is no way back from reflectiveness.[1] Here, a clear declaration for Critical Pedagogy is helpful to support a transformative praxis consisting of transformative dialectical learning[2] in which means are not made absolute, and in which the limits of reason are determined by reason as the central notion of an enlightenment whose educational motto would be to strengthen the human being while clarifying things.[3]

Critical Pedagogy shares with Critical Theory the conviction "that all educational processes are essentially historical"[4] and the "denial of the existence of a transcendental principle of personality formation":

> Still, the educational aim of the consistent and self-identical person as such is maintained in Critical Theory. It obtains the status not of an actual aim but of a counter-factual ideal. This is what 'emancipation' really seems to be about: the realization of an educational ideal which under current circumstances in society is denied. Inevitably, as in general Critical Theory, the problem now becomes whether we can find some force or principle *immanent* in history which, although not guaranteed to yield the desired outcome, may at least guide our actions towards the realization of emancipation.[5]

This force or principle may be found in the understanding that 'the Enlightenment' has changed the conditions for 'enlightenment'. These conditions have become more realistic and stronger, particularly through an understanding of reason which today has to be taken as the ability to withstand those problems it does itself create; it cannot escape its historicality.[6]

Essentialist and contextualist modes of pedagogical thought are demonstrated in the teaching of essentialist-contextualist, epistemologies aimed at a greater curriculum-consciousness of teacher and pupil. A new and greater curriculum-consciousness could be the foundation to, finally, taming the power of educational institutions and teachers. Though the project of modernity is based on the idea of freedom from traditional authorities, modernist institutions are known to operate in contradictory ways, "espousing at the level of rhetoric, but fostering heteronomy, discipline and oppression in practice."[7]

Our final conclusion is that a "circle of congruence" of essentialist and contextualist thought (abstraction and application of knowledge) and practice (consciousness of curriculum) can save us the unnecessary but fashionable categorization of educational thought and practice into modernist and postmodernist attitudes.

> Let us understand 'postmodern' with Terry Eagleton as a style of thought which is suspicious of classical notions of truth, reason, identity, and objectivity, of the ideal of universal progress or emancipation, of single frameworks, grand narratives or ultimate grounds of explanation. Against these Enlightenment norms, it sees the world as contingent, ungrounded, diverse, unstable, indeterminate, a set of disunified cultures or interpretations which breed a degree of skepticism about the objectivity of truth, history, and norms, the giveness of natures and the coherence of identities.[8]

and 'modern' with J.F. Lyotard as

> any science that legitimates itself with reference to a metadiscourse of this kind making an explicit appeal to some grand narrative, such as the dialectics of spirit, the hermeneutics of meaning, the emancipation of the rational or working subject, or the creation of wealth.[9]

In our circle of congruence of thought and practice we should be able to approach the problem from an angle of conciliation, interpreting postmodernism as a possible trend or tendency within modernism rather than a general state-of-the-world that has superseded it.[10]

Is it not so that human history has experienced modernity several times albeit with different forms and content? Though we tend to attach modernity to the Enlightenment[11] and the Industrial Revolution, humankind has faced upheavals before (for instance, the breakdown of the traditional virtues in Athens at the time of Socrates, the decline of the Hellenistic world, the end of metaphysics at the time of Kant). Such an upheaval

> results in a specific attitude toward reality which, to differentiate it from a subjective state, Foucault calls an ethos. In a modernity-crisis, a taken-for-granted understanding of reality ceases to function as a shared background in terms of

> which people can orient and justify their activity and the modernist response is heroically and lucidly to face up to the collapse of the old order.[12]

In a circle of congruence of thought and practice we are compelled to search for the structure of human finitude, the universal in the singular, and the serious in the ironic:

> On the one hand, the anti-thinkers, on the basis of a historical theory of the human subject as empty desire constituted by the arbitrary play of signifiers, condemn seriousness and insist that everyone be relentlessly ironic. On the other hand, the heroic defenders of seriousness, on the basis of a theory of communication, condemn what they consider irresponsible irony, and, in an exasperated tone, seek to remind everyone of his duty to conform to the universal imperative implicit in all speech acts.[13]

Not only Foucault resisted both these philosophical, universalizing positions. We are here not celebrating a postmodern plurality of identities and fragmentation, nor do we consider postmodernism being rationalized through an apologetics of banality and conformity, rather we think that our circle of congruence would be more in keeping with Kant's task of using critical reason maturely and with Foucault's idea of an interpretive analytics, viz.

> (1) to describe and interpet our current practices so as to understand what aspects of modernity we have to accept as inescapable; (2) to characterize the sense, diffusely manifest in the practices of some epochs that in some pervasive way things have gone awry... (3) to articulate further a widely shared sense that the promise of the enlightenment has yet to be fulfilled; (4) to go beyond thinkers and anti-thinkers in taking a stand toward the present that does not legislate empty universal norms but encourages conflicts of interpretation; (5) and to go beyond Foucault in rhetorically strengthening the post-enlightenment practices that are positive, such as many of our technological, legal and medical advantages, and in identifying and preserving pre-enlightenment practices which have so far escaped rationalization and normalization.[14]

As long as we are using reason maturely (as a capability to get on well with what remains unintelligible without giving up the demand for intelligibility[15]) in our desire and need to establish pluralities of truth (and none of the postmodernists has shed it or else they would not have been able to come out with their elaborate texts on texts), we are tempted to universalize our findings so that even a completely deconstructed text is believed to be the result of truth—and any truth, even the most fleeting and fragmented, is for a minute or so held as universal, but not necessarily the whole truth. This 'whole truth' is simply not desirable in emancipatory education where knowledge should dissolve domination and where ideas may become more universal.[16]

The ongoing discussion of modernism versus postmodernism has certainly enriched the debate about the aims and purpose of education and has given the philosophy of education a focus which is not shying away from the historical and political implications for the functioning of education as a system in society.[17] My sympathy, as this inquiry has made clear, is with the thought that the modernist attitude is more appropriate for our work as teachers as long as we have not achieved a (re)conciliatory plateau as mentioned above. This attitude is constantly placing the human being in the centre, affirming a grand design and advancing an overarching explanation of the world, and believing in the possibility of emancipation.[18]

The meaning of modernism demands of education to aim at the formation of the "whole person".[19] It should also deal with, what a postmodernist attitude signifies, the loneliness of moral choice, the illusions of certainties, and a modesty about the aims of schooling. A modernist attitude will be a protection against an "anti-intellectual education ideology that has raised commonsense beliefs to the status of self-authorizing truth."[20]

We may hold that a postmodernist attitude is nothing but the modern mind taking a hard look at itself, at its past work and its condition, and thus is to rethink our understanding of the emancipatory vision of education.[21] This surely cannot be regarded as a threat to emancipatory education but rather as "an indispensable aid to the future accomplishments of its goals."[22] In doing so, we are not helping the cause by simply attacking the negative characteristics of a postmodernist culture from being chaotic to showing scant regard for social responsibility[23], instead we are advised to reply to fundamental postmodernist critiques within our educational domain, and eventually use them for our emancipatory view of education which, ultimately, stems from Kant's foundationalist philosophy—"a philosophy designed to show that the Enlightenment concept of the rationally autonomous subject did not simply apply to a particular culture or society but was grounded in *a priori* truths about the 'universal essence' of human nature itself."[24] We dare assume that this universal essence of human nature is the force which can bind thinkers as diverse as, for example, Gandhi and Habermas in their shared "emancipatory élan"[25] to reintegrate ethics and politics and to seek "to reclaim the freedom of autonomy of the individual from the technocrats of social power".[26]

Today's critics may be justified in their disapproval of the overriding success of the three pillars of modernity, science, capitalism and liberal democracy, and their corresponding abiding themes of Western civilization, progress and universality.[27] Nevertheless, we cannot reject the view that all the freedoms we enjoy today and ought to be obliged to pass on are fruits of the Enlightenment, and that "it was not the Enlightenment that failed... but rather those who were appointed its guardians."[28] In the benevolent optimism of the Enlightenment with its constant values of reason, freedom, truth and justice we may find our "*sole hope* of making history and in so doing of carrying on the one truly humane business: lending meaning to the meaningless."[29]

On the other hand, our circle of congruence must not underestimate that any discourse of modernity is signified, if not suffering, from the time-lag

> that emerges in the tension between the epocal 'event' of modernity as the symbol of the continuity of progress, and the interruptive temporality of the sign of the present, the contingency of modern times that Habermas has aptly described as its 'forward gropings and shocking encounters'. In this 'time' of repetition there circulates a contingent tension within modernity: a tension between the *pedagogy* of the symbols of progress, historicism, modernization, homogeneous

> empty time. The narcissism of organic culture, the onanistic search for the origins of race, and what I shall call the 'sign of the present': the performativity of discursive practice, the récites of the everyday, the repetition of the empirical, the ethics of self-enactment, the iterative signs that mark the non-synchronic *passages* of time in the archives of the new".[30]

It is true that we are caught in this temporal caesura, but this is not reason enough not to see scepticism as a rather ingeniously complementary in the peaceful struggle for enlightened humanism in a genuine competition with a postmodernist purpose to refine the former.[31]

Let me finally come back to this humanist quest which cannot be destroyed. Whatever critiques we inflict upon each other, we cannot, as William James said, "weed out the human contribution": "Our nouns and adjectives are all humanized heirlooms, and in the theories we build them in, the inner order and arrangement is wholly dictated by human considerations, intellectual consistency being one of them." And he asserts since we create the subjects we also create the predicates.[32]

May be Julian Huxley's 'evolutionary humanism' is well-equipped to give emancipatory education a new life and direction. Unfortunately, emancipatory education was abandoned by many of us (including this writer) after the euphoria of the 60s and 70s about the political power of education. Huxley reminds us in his essays written before this time of exuberance, that in order to reunify one's life (after the catastrophies and chaos of the first half of this century) we have to do this within a framework of a satisfactory idea system[33] which he calls 'humanism' because such an idea-system

> can only be based on our understanding of man, and his relations with the rest of the environment. It must be focused on man as an organism, though one with unique properties. It must be organized around the facts and ideas of evolution, taking account of the discovery that man is part of a comprehensive evolutionary process, and cannot avoid playing a decisive role in it.[34]

This evolutionary humanism

> is necessarily unitary instead of dualistic, affirming the unity of mind and body; universal instead of particularist, affirming

> the continuity of man with the rest of life, and of life with the rest of the universal; naturalistic instead of supernaturalist, affirming the unity of the spiritual and the material; and global instead of divisive, affirming the unity of all mankind.[35]

And then he strikes a chord with those who want to bring together the largely unutilized resources of our knowledge by warning that this idea-system humanism

> will have nothing to do with Absolutes, including absolute truth, absolute morality, absolute perfection, and absolute authority, but insists that we can find standards to which our actions and our aims can properly be related. It affirms knowledge and understanding can be increased, that conduct and social organization can be improved, and that more desirable direction for individual and social development can be found. As the overriding aim of evolving man, it is driven to reject power, or mere numbers of people, or efficiency, or material exploitation, and to envisage greater fulfilment and fuller achievement of his true goal.[36]

We have here certainly to accept the weakening of our basic Kantian position of *a priori* truths but do so in the conviction that Huxley's view is a more educative one than Kant's. In practical education, we have to deal with growth and development, with incompletes within a vision, and with our own faults in relation to the right knowledge and the proper ways of educating others. We can only deal with varied excellence in which teachers "must resist the imposition of all dogmatisms, including their own". They will have to remember "that cultural and individual diversity is precious in itself, and will strive for vivifying variety and against monotonous mediocrity". But above all "they will hold fast to the humanist vision of variety in unity, and will endeavour to provide a common ground of thought action, and a unitary vision and framework of ideas which all human variants can share".[37]

In our attempt to uphold a humanist essentialism and contextualism in education, we argue that the notion of a normative core of knowledge ('the idea') *and* the demand for a radical analysis of reality ('the facts') should be welcomed as the two-pronged strategy for pedagogies to keep their identities, to reduce their differences in conflicts of interpretation, and to strive together for a maximum amount of factual information while providing comprehension as the unifying element of any curriculum.

Pedagogy is not philosophy; the latter can afford to be irreconciliable, the former not. Philosophy can be 'left alone', a mere shrugging of our shoulders, a gadfly which we can afford to neglect; pedagogy has to be done the next day in class and hence forces us at least to attempt a circle of knowledge formation which is produced in a discourse of reason.

One imminent quality of a discourse of reason is its openness and openendedness to a critique of reason which, ultimately, does not preclude the coexistence of 'the word' understood in a multitude of ways. I consider this circle as educational modernity, and thus still a project of the Enlightenment—indeed one which will *always* be unfinished.

Referrences

1. See to this Susan Mendus, 1992.
2. See to this Helmut Peukert, 1993.
3. So the title of the very stimulating book by Hartmut von Hentig, 1985.
4. Willem L. Wardekker/Siebren Miedema, 1997, p. 49.
5. Ibid., p. 51.
6. Hartmut von Hentig, 1985, p. 38. See to this also Jürgen Habermas, 1989, p. 201: ".... it is precisely in Germany that the self-critique of the Enlightenment is as old as the Enlightenment itself. Anyone who did not know the limits of the intellect (Verstand) was always considered irrational. If the intellect is inflated to the totality and usurps the place of reason (Vernunft), the mind loses its capacity to reflect on the limits of the intellectual activity. Thus it is of the very nature of the Enlightenment to enlighten itself about itself, and about the harm that it does. Only when this fact is repressed can the counter-Enlightenment present itself as enlightenment about the Enlightenment."
7. John Quicke, 1996, p. 364.
8. Quoted in Colin Mooers, 1997, pp. 58-59.
9. Quoted in Paul Smeyers, 1995, p. 116.
10. John Quicke, 1996, p. 364.

11. The Enlightenment is generally described as "a movement whose major intellectual impulses were critical, analytic, scientific, mechanistic and anti-metaphysical. Epistemologically, the Enlightenment is normally seen as sensationalist and associationist, with a straight line running from Locke to the outright skepticism of Hume. The deductive reasoning characteristic of the seventeenth century metaphysicians like Spinoza and Leibniz was replaced by empiricist deduction. Politically, the Enlightenment is usually associated with social contract theory, individualism, natural right theory, and the pursuit of self-interest, rather than the search for community or the justification of hierarchy." (Martin Jay: *Marxism and Totality: The Adventures of a Concept from Lukacs to Habermas*, 1984, p. 30, as quoted in Geoffrey Galt Harpham, 1994, p. 531.) As to India, Paulos Mar Gregorios (1989) is of the opinion that the two twin children of the Enlightenment, Marxism and Liberalism, are still guiding today's India in terms of political culture. In this book, he does not hide his admiration for Europe's achievement, but nevertheless puts up the idea of an Indian approach to Enlightenment which he sees, eventually, emerging from an analysis of the debates between Hindu and Buddhist philosophers of the 4th to the 10th centuries. Its product, a Buddhist realism and secularism, would not be a copy of Europe's "unexamined realism" and therefore not "un-Indian" (p. 125); instead, it would be an emancipation from "naive realism" and the first step to an authentic Indian identity. It would be a system of thought which is based on "enlightened human reasons" that is "illumined by a trans-conscious experience of samyaksambodhi" (p. 126). The major question in such a Buddhist realism would be 'What is the true nature of this world of things which confronts us?' a question which was unanswered by, for example, Kant. Paulos Mar Gregorios is, however, far away from seeing in postmodernism a viable alternative to Enlightenment and labels it simply as a "mood" (1997, p. 84), though, in these last notes he argues also sharply against the European Enlightenment as a "tyrannical-absolute quest to master the world" (p. 86).

12. Hubert L. Dreyfus/Paul Rabinow, 1989, p. 117.

13. *Ibid.*, pp. 118-119.

14. *Ibid.* pp. 120-121.

15. Hartmut von Hentig, 1985, p. 11.

16. Against these and other Enlightenment maxims Max Horkheimer and Theodor Adorno have vehemently argued in their *Dialectic of Enlightenment* (originally published in 1944). Just for illustration, here some of their verdicts (from an excerpt under the title "The Concept

of Enlightenment", pp. 44-50, in Carolyn Merchant, ed., 1996): "Enlightenment is totalitarian." (p. 46) "Abstraction, the tool of Enlightenment, treats its objects as did fate, the notion of which it rejects: it liquidates them." (p. 47) "The universality of ideas as developed by discursive logic, domination in the conceptual sphere, is raised up on the basis of actual domination." (p. 48) Knowledge becomes "the dissolution of domination. But in the face of such a possibility and in the service of the present age, Enlightenment becomes wholesale deception of the masses." (p. 50).

17. Besides those referred to earlier, the following are useful analyses: Dennis Carlson, 1995; Michael Peters, 1995, Mike Cole/Dave Hill, 1995; Mike Cole/Dave Hill/ Glenn Rikowski, 1997; Nigel Blake, 1992; Nigel Blake, 1997.
18. Paul Standish, 1995, p. 125.
19. *Ibid.*, p. 124.
20. Wilfred Carr, 1995, p. 78.
21. *Ibid*,, p. 79.
22. *Ibid.*, pp. 89-90.
23. Referring to an overview in Jean-Francois Lyotard's classic *The Postmodern Condition: A Report on Knowledge* (1984, pp. 121-123), Jim Collins (1989, p. 132) lists—by arguing sharply against those who criticize postmodernism—as other negative characteristics: eclecticism absence of aesthetic criteria, sheer heterogeneity, random difference, undecidable effectivity, absence of any great collective project, and de-historicized culture.
24. Wilfred Carr, 1995, pp. 79-80.
25. Fred Dallnayr, 1992, p. 433.
26. Thomas Pantham, 1987, p. 306.
27. See to this David R. Gress, 1997, pp. 538-539.
28. Jean Améry, 1984, p. 136.
29. Ibid. p. 140.
30. Homi K. Bhaba, 1995, p. 245.
31. See to the concept of "struggle" Max Weber, 1978, pp. 85-89.
32. William James, 1975, p. 166.
33. Julian Huxley (1964, p. 120) uses *ideas* "in a broad and loose sense to cover beliefs and values as well as general and scientific concepts. Ideas are real phenomena, part of man's psycho-social equipment.

Before new factual knowledge can become effective, it must be organized, incorporated in, or related to an idea. Ideas, of course, grow out of our experiences, both external and internal, but differ a great deal in what may be called their scientific or objective validation. Where detailed and scientific validation is meagre or not available, ideas can still exact strong psycho-social effects: for instance, the idea of monotheism, or of personal salvation through religious faith or sacred ritual. But in the long run those ideas will prevail which are scientifically validated and are backed by a mass of established factual knowledge".

34. *Ibid.*, p. 73.

35. *Ibid.*, p. 73.

36. *Ibid.*, pp. 73-74.

37. *Ibid.*, p. 135.

38. But I would also agree with Axel Honneth who, in an interview with Peter Osborne, opines that Habermas, to whom we have referred so often in an affirmative way, may be too narrow in describing mechanisms of understanding in human beings only via language. He suggests to go back to philosophical anthropology in order "to have a broader approach to certain transcendental features of human beings" and a "stronger foundation...for the normative critique of our society". This foundation would be methodologically more disputable for a critical theory and less universalizable in its normative criteria, but, eventually, fuller in humanistic understanding nonetheless. (Peter Osborne, 1996, p. 100).

7

Synopsis

The problem taken up in this inquiry into the philosophy of education is that teachers tend not to clarify the meaning of the knowledge they teach and take too much of it on trust. They do not like to ask the question, what are the rules for the use of this or that knowledge. Instead, they teach knowledge as part of a ritual which is meant to be taken for granted and prefer to operate with vague but nevertheless fixed ideas about the nature and use of knowledge.

I

Epistemologies dominate ordinary educational thought which is thinking about education without permanently reflecting the process of education. Epistemologies of this thought tend to be pragmatic, linear and geared towards immediate applicability. They are rarely pro-enlightenment but implicitly postmodern. These epistemologies are often hidden in the routine of educational strategies and techniques and not always known to the protagonists themselves. They are also determined by socio-economic relations with a thrust on conservative ideas. This status must not be understood as the modern condition of educational thought.

II

The modern condition of educational thought is the acceptance of the dialogic relationship between theory and practice in which epistemologies create reflective educational thought. These epistemologies are then contributions to teach within histories of ideas.

Theory is immanent in concepts which may be called 'essentials', practice in concepts which may be called 'contextuals'.

Essentials and contextuals can be represented by the same word but do not mean the same at the same time. Since human activity is temporal, the two cannot be the same on the level of time. An essential represents an idea which is thought necessary for the purposeful functioning of education. A contextual also represents an idea but one which is nearer to the 'real' nature of a thing because this thing has been explored, experienced, reflected upon, and finally become part of one's social consciousness.

Consequently, there are two modes of thought, the essentialist and the contextualist. The essentialist mode is characterized by future-orientation, weak historical rooting and little social analysis. This mode is usually in favour of a fixed canon of knowledge. The contextualist mode is characterized by grappling with everyday's social and educational reality, its historical roots and a number of socializing factors. It tends to be ready to add new knowledge to curricula.

The modern condition of educational thought depends on both these modes of thought. Together they can construct epistemologies which are signified by a healthy scepticism and tentative answers, in other words, by a scientific temperament. These epistemologies would then be of a robust humanist radicalism, viz. to doubt, to accept the humanness of everything, to believe in the liberating power of truth, and to perceive reality dialectically.

III

In ordinary educational thought we tend to turn to the essentialist mode of thought, not so much because of our belief in universal goods but because of the fact that this mode does not, at first sight, advocate change—and change on many levels is virtually anathema to many teachers. This is, however, a wrong understanding of the function of an essential and its mode of thought for no concept can be pure, i.e., without content. Any concept by its very existence is a concept of and therefore a concept with regard to something and thus contains an inherent element of change per se. Furthermore, much speaks for the fact that there is no interest-free, i.e., neutral concept and use of a concept. If this is so, then even an essential cannot always be an essential but has turned at some stage into something more contextual.

We can now speak of essentialism representing the essentialist mode of thought and contextualism the contextualist mode. Essentialism is here denoted as the process of construction of a grand educational design which is to be built on universally affirmed ideas. Complementary to this, contextualism considers educational thought to be a continuous pedagogic reflection on ideas and practices pertaining to the present human condition. Essentialism and contextualism will have both to be used in order to arrive at a humanistic conception of education that relies on the unavoidable presupposition of communication to guarantee transformative dialectical learning.

IV

If essentialism is not counterposed by analyses of contemporary social and educational reality, then educational practices will be mostly in favour of those who have the means to manipulate essentials, truth would not anymore be the correspondence of objective reality, and reason would degenerate into dull formality. This would support statuses quo in education and suit the guild of teachers who have a known history of complicity with the powers to be. This would support dominant classes in society and a repressive state in the forms of socio-cultural hegemonization and socio-political authoritarianism.

But contextualism also needs the controlling and guiding force of essentialism, mainly for two reasons: first, lifeworlds in all their individual and societal context are far too complex for even the most precise and detailed contextual analysis to cover—that is why essentialist thought can and must provide direction. And second, lifeworlds continually recreate visions and Great Ideas to sustain ideals which are necessary for education to have a purpose and to be justified.

The modern condition of educational thought is demonstrated by a definite connection between essentialist and contextualist modes of thought. This connection is the continuous process of transformation of essentials into contextuals and vice versa. This process of transformation or pedagogical code-switching takes place before, during, after, and over the entire period of an educational practice, however hardly in a sudden flash but in a discourse which can be taking place with others or within oneself. Both concepts and modes of thought gain and lose in this process of perpetual redefinition. Gaining and losing in a communicative action on the meeting ground of a Grand Morality and the cultural analysis of a decentred educational environment occurs in the realms of relevance, validity, clarity, and rigour.

Teachers and pupils who realize that they are part of such a transformation through their reflection-in and reflection-on action respectively contribute to education as emancipation and a growing curriculum-consciousness. Their emancipation is permanent reflection and participation, placed through language in an intersubjectivity of unconstrained agreement. In other words, it is the application of the 'discourse theory of truth' guided by the idea that agreement is the immanent telos of language.

V

It is not necessary to categorize educational thought neatly into modernist and postmodernist. Rather it is argued that simultaneously the notion of a normative core and the demand for a radical analysis of reality be upheld in order to overcome conflicts of interpretation. There is a circle of congruence produced in the discourse of an essentialist synthesis and a contextualist analysis which is perhaps allowing enlightenment to be realized but always as an unfinished project.

Humanism is conceived as the main frame for this project.

PART—II

TWO CASE STUDIES

8

Multiculturalism—A Critique of an Educational Idea

Tamil Nadu hosts on its western border the Kodaikanal International School (KIS), a reputed seat of international education. The school was founded as a missionary school in 1901 and changed to its present form in 1974. It claims to follow the ideals of a Christian and multicultural pedagogy for its c. 550 pupils from kindergarten to 12th grade (roughly half of the pupils and staff are Christians). Its international character is, however, limited because its main elements are an amalgam of the tenets of a crude pragmatism and the constraints of a one-truth claim in the Christian faith. In case of a conflict, such an outlook does invite people to regard the latter more important than the former.

KIS as a "Christian Multicultural School" is in the midst of a well-known controversy, viz. to decide what multiculturalism is or could be. It appears as though its Board of Management wants the school to follow a form of multiculturalism which Smolicz has declared as "dominant monism", in which one dominant culture (here, religious) group determines the norms of living together. Maybe it is hoped by some that in practice the school would follow another interpretation of multiculturalism which would imply "that individuals from both majority and minority backgrounds would have the opportunity to make use of more than one culture in their everyday lives, be it in language, family life, social manners, ideology, or the higher spheres of culture, such as literature and art."[1] But whoever has worked in the school for a longer time and has carefully observed the styles and work of its staff and pupils knows that this interpretation does not fully match the reality of the school. Instead, the school policy *appreciates* the "specific cultural identity' and *affirms* the "unity of mankind—but "without losing its global and Christian character".[2]

There are two presuppositions which lie at the base of my thinking on the topic. First, I prefer any school to be secular, non-capitalistic, non-racial and egalitarian. By secular I mean that school should not be tied up to the values and practices of one religion alone; by non-capitalistic I mean that a school should not be regarded as an institution which is a profit-making undertaking or which prepares pupils, at any cost, for capitalistic societies alone; and by non-racial and egalitarian I mean that a school should help facilitate the functioning of a non-racial and egalitarian community in its own fold first. Second, I think that any ideology, also the one in the form of a religion, is based on the particular interests of those who have established this ideology and not necessarily on the interests of those who are exposed to it. In other words, I look upon any ideology first as an instrument of power which then becomes the essence of the structure of an institution which, in turn, reinforces its particular ideology.[3]

I

Even after years of daily teaching (which could have been a source of delusion save for the excellent teaching and learning conditions at KIS), I do hold the view that the pursuit of truth on all academic levels is the salient feature of education. It is, however, pointless for me, not only as a teacher, to start this search for truth from a platform of faith since "there is no reason to suppose any religion true".[4] Whatever faith we take, it does not allow us to accept any other spiritual perception as equal. Various historical and situational forms of truth in the realm of mind become then less true. The more rigid a faith is, and as a matter of fact any faith has to be rigid by virtue of its definition, the more fruitless it is for a society—if this society aims at being open and egalitarian. That is so because any faith contains elements of thought which tend to perpetuate the status quo of mind.

Any faith advocates an all-embracing truth while its followers adopt occasionally rather down-to-earth techniques. These techniques are packed, at times, either in the brutal means of force or the soft language of caring and sharing as means of persuasion. These techniques either violently or elegantly close the doors to any other truth under the pretext that universals are the same everywhere, which they have to be as a matter of fact by virtue of their name. But this says only something about the desire of people for universals, nothing however, about the objective reality of existence which is, I maintain, a reality of particulars which we try to approximate to the status of universals. The existence of universals cannot be taken for granted and is difficult to demonstrate since mental processes, attitudes and values, for example also those constituting force, caring and sharing[5], are concepts with a history, which means any concept in life or life itself, is changeable and transitory.[6]

Pupils brought up in a tradition of faith have no reason to regard knowledge in other subjects and areas of life as less reliable. Once they are taught and made to believe that there is, for example, a god which cannot be proved, why should they then develop critical thought about, for instance, the thesis that man strives for power or that red is red and not blue. Once we have forced beliefs down their throats, we cannot, in the next minute, expect pupils to follow the path of logical rigour and strict reasoning. Thus, giving a school a moral base through a common faith might be useful for guidelines of how to live together but not necessarily true. This is also the dilemma of KIS with its heterogenous composition of pupils and staff on the one side and a clearly chalked out form of an official ethics based on (a particular form of) Christianity on the other. This is not at all a new dilemma for people who do not follow their own intellect but like to work within the frame of an emotive-intellectual structure provided by others. Already in 1662, in his "Treaties on the Improvement of the Understanding", Spinoza warned of this "ignorance of the causes by which they are conditioned".[7]

The question now arises, how much of standpointlessness (as contrary to faith) towards truth can a school afford without disintegrating into moral lawlessness? Some may find complete standpointlessness a plausible answer because this would allow anyone to breathe fresh air and to follow a calculated rootlessness which would certainly be at the expense of losing the social warmth of a like-minded group which anyway could not exist in such a climate. The other extreme could be seen in a set of religious values based on faith which would provide one with a feeling of righteousness and knowledge of what to do when, certainly then at the expense of one's ability to be intellectually open to other ideas and to examine them critically and either to adopt, adapt or reject them.

Though I do prefer from an anarchic position the first answer, I have to admit that it would not possibly work in a school since education can practically not function in utter standpointlessness, if this value exists at all, which I doubt. Here again a warning by Spinoza may prevent us from going overboard: "Will cannot be called a free cause, but only a necessary cause. In the mind there is no absolute or free will; but the mind is determined to wish this or that by cause, which has also been determined by another cause, and this last by another cause, and soon to infinity."[8] In our words, even to represent the value of standpointlessness is to have a value and can, thus, not be standpointlessness any more. Children and youth (and adults too) seem to need, intellectually and emotionally, a graded system of growth, a way which allows them to develop gradually. Hardly ever do people grow mature enough to enjoy confusion on a mental plane which is so often the origin of creative knowledge and situational truth though. Instead, they need stable and regular modes of behaviour and learning and living, they need anchors on their ways of understanding life. How to equip them with these, is one of the age-old problems of education. Humankind has resorted to all kinds of answers and experiments with the result that our world is not at all better in morals than any other before, at least according to the knowledge we can derive from recorded history.

Nonetheless, one element of education is hope. But shall we really expose pupils to a system which is based on 'might, 'ought' and 'should'; or shall we ask them to experience the cold of a metaphysical position which promises certainty only after a long time of searching—if at all? I prefer, again from an anarchic point of view, the less educative position, but, again, also know that it is impractical to overestimate human nature. This is why I suggest that we only minimize the one-faith direction in education in order to give pupils and teachers alike a fair chance of perceiving more than situational truth, i.e., knowledge which is open to discovery and which is thereby in "correspondence with objective reality".[9]

Put into practice, this idea would, in the end, be the seed for a secular school in which not only is every faith represented but also pursued on an *equal* basis, i.e., giving each the same chance and attention in its daily routine.[10] This is a compromise and not at all a 'pure' solution which would lie either in complete faithlessness or in a strict one-faith system. If it is true what some assert (I disagree) that all the great spiritual ideas of humankind are found in any one of the great world religions (whatever a great world religion is), then there is no risk for a school like KIS in accepting this compromise. On the other hand, this argument would also offer the conclusion that, then, the teaching of one of the religious systems would be sufficient indeed in order to get to 'the truth' and to establish a body of homogeneous knowledge and morals. But then we would simply ignore the vast differences in background and social environment of many of the pupils and staff of KIS. If we compromise, then we have at least tried to avoid the monolythic truth of one system of faith and knowledge and would be much more open to the goal of quest for truth. I am afraid that the present position of KIS is in-between which is unfortunate because it signifies an intellectual muddle.[11]

A secular school could, instead, develop a style of work which may encourage pupils and staff to follow their respective faiths which seems to be a psychological need, and at the same time foster a healthy aloofness from dogmatics. By this it may perhaps get a bit nearer to the lofty ideal of multiculturalism which is nothing but a euphemism for a must to live together in a multicultural situation because of circumstances. I am convinced that living together in such a multinational situation is regarded by many as a necessary evil and not, for example, a stepping stone to world peace. It seems that the desire of human beings to stick to their own creed and stock is so overwhelming that alternatives are hardly liked but only accepted.[12]

It is interesting to observe that the most frequent appeals to multicultural understanding come often from those who have never gone through the daily living-together experience apart from the usual patronizing relationships which are so common among the orders of international aid and development workers, tourists, foster parents, employees of international organizations, missionaries, and politicians. The liberal ideas of integration and assimilation which might be accepted as major constituents of multiculturalism are hardly put into practice and if, then usually under the roof of a minimum needs programme diluting them even further. This minimum is for some a common language or a common faith which satisfies a harmony on the surface that, however, seeps away the deeper we dig into the structures of personalities and institutions.[13]

Here arises now the question, who needs this kind of harmony or who needs this kind of lulling family feeling? From my experience in international development work and international schooling, I dare say that it is needed most by those who know that they are dependent on it, i.e., those who profit from it and whose status would not allow them to be around if they reflected it ruthlessly. Striving for harmony can be an attempt to justify one's behaviour and position. That is why salesmen of harmony are trying at all costs to avoid conflicts which could only land them into trouble, even to the extent of questioning their very existence in the international field. I find this situation represented at KIS too, and cannot see in this situation specifically multicultural knowledge and truth—if they exist at all.

II

If the concept of truth has not been clarified for the education practiced at KIS and is, therefore, no help to arrive at a sounder concept of multiculturalism, what then can help achieve this? Not a few of us working in the multicultural field think that what we call, more out of helplessness than preciseness, 'multicultural culture' might be the panacea. In my opinion, this is not only false but also dangerous because a simplistic understanding of multicultural culture is aggravating the intellectual muddle and is in turn supporting a political attitude which I like to contribute to the idea of colonialism.

I do not try here to give a new definition of culture; anthropologists and sociologists have laid their hands upon this numerous times before. One thing seems to have emerged out of their attempts: culture cannot only be understood as art and literature and so forth but as a way of life stressing more than ever the mundane aspects of life. I like to adopt this broad understanding because it then becomes clear that the efforts by some at KIS to introduce Indian culture through the occasional

Indian dance, theatre and music programme will not change the 'Western' way of life which prevails amongst pupils and staff, quite in tune with global economic and political developments. Nor will a rather helpless social experience programme have any impact on this since the perception of reality will not change while visiting or patronizing poor people. On the contrary, they will establish amongst pupils and staff the feeling that their own way of life is certainly better and that the poor, downtrodden, under-privileged and so on should be lifted to their level. This experience will hardly ever support the idea that something in the way we live might be wrong, as perhaps seen by the poor and suppressed.

KIS, in my opinion, is not able to and in no need to Indianize. But is it, on the other hand, capable to multiculturalize? I do not think so because the direction what is good and what is bad for the education practised at KIS has been ascertained in the past when the school was an all-white missionary establishment, and I have not seen major changes in attitudes towards morals and norms which form the culture of living together in the school, whether it is the relationship between boys and girls, between white and non-white staff, between Christians and non-Christians, or between professional and non-professional staff. It appears as though these foundations for living together are only clear to, and complied with, by some of the pupils and staff. For others, it is either adjustment, indifference or silence, a situation which Paulo Freire has time and again analysed as the colonial and oppressive "cultural invasion" which leads to a "culture of silence".[14]

But maybe we should see it also as the other way round, i.e., changes have occurred within the purview of those who had the influence and power to accept or reject suggestions. Maybe these changes were implemented with the good of all in mind. Maybe people believed that by this they protected the school's foundation which to them was sacrosanct. Maybe this was as it has to be when you want to build up an institution and anyone of us would do the same if we were in a similar position. But maybe this does not mean either that qualitatively major avenues of thought and action were opened to all involved in this process.

We should also see the situation of KIS critically in terms of India's colonial history without which our presence in India cannot be understood. Four historical phases can be outlined: first, the phase of oriental despotism, which was the pretext for the British "to restore order" in the India of the 18th century; second, the phase of village republics and castes which was utilized by the British for a theory of rule "from London down into every village" and was, at the same time, a convenient justification for collecting taxes; third, the feudal phase in the middle of the 19th century with the British on top, ruling under God and Divine Providence; and fourth, the phase of competition and conspiracy in the last decades of the 19th century arguing that India as a land of groups was prone to a Hobbsian war of all against all—if it were not for the strong rule of the British.[15] I think it is not improper to add a modern phase which may be called "domination by cooperation", and in which business, aid and services are used, sometimes unknowingly, to rule.[16] India seems to be in the midst of this phase as we know, amongst other things, from her precarious role as a regular borrower in the international money market and as a host of the not-so-independent charity and service organizations at the NGO-level. The multiculturalness at KIS represents, even today at the end of the 20th century, still traces of all the colonial phases in the minds and practices of some staff and pupils.

Many in the school have accepted complacency as their major form of thinking on education and politics. They seem to be satisfied with a potpourri of superficial feelings which are often related to the concept of a family, by this playing down that a family, probably in whatever part of the world, but certainly in India[17], can also be the seat of tense conflicts and brutal fights. But the potpourri is, of course, easier to digest when people come together from several parts of the world. To build up an egalitarian organization under these circumstances is trying and would be much more difficult. The 'family-ideology' does not deserve, however, to be labelled as multiculturalism because it lacks honesty and straightforwardness on the one hand, and depth and comprehensiveness on the other. However, honesty from teachers and pupils is, rightly so, demanded in the classroom accepting, at least here, the supremacy of openness to any question in the realm of mind as a fundamental principle in the pursuit of truth. In practice though, a track is followed which is too often paved by others. Rarely is a critical situation, for example, in one's own multicultural life, taken as a reason for a social analysis which then could explain why conflicts have come about, or why one follows this pathway and not another.

Why all this? The answer is simple and twofold. This hanging on to the old is, firstly, not intellectually demanding and can, secondly, be executed in the same old structures of white on the top and brown at the bottom, though with a lot more cosmetics as cover up than in the past. This means that the power structure need not be changed, or only marginally. All you have to do is to co-opt people and give them the illusion that they are part of this power structure and tell them once in a while how good they are and how well they contribute to the family. That what is good is, of course, defined by the power holders. This is an age-old game played to perfection at the time when countries of the 'Third World' were under foreign rule; it is a modern variation of the infamous British divide-and-rule.

There is one major flaw in this thought though. The error is that the advocates of neo-colonialism think and hope that the old rule can last for ever. It is known from history that rulers tend to think like this—whether they were absolute or enlightened rulers. The reality is quite otherwise. Under the veneer of smooth functioning, there is a strong desire that a new system has to be built up. People want to see their own culture of living together represented in this new system; they want to see their own aspirations being voiced and taken seriously—only to end up, if they get the opportunity, as another set of rulers.

Despite this rather pessimistic cycle, languages would be a good beginning for a change since they represent genuine thoughts and emotions of people. In communication, no degree of excitement whatsoever for strange customs, be they incense sticks or eating with sticks, can replace the significance of learning languages. To be fascinated or charmed by the 'exotic' without penetrating its deeper meaning will never create a platform of common understanding.

But what is being done concerning languages at KIS? Virtually nothing worth an international school and its immense potential. Here I do not mean only a modest English-as-a-Second-Language programme and the generally low rating of foreign languages in the curriculum. Here I also mean the attitude towards languages which are known or spoken on campus. I think I do not exaggerate in stating that not many of the teaching staff are involved in learning the other's language. This is more revealing when we take a look at the top-bottom structure of the school. Hardly anyone on the top is learning a language other than English. But on the other hand, there are quite a few people at the bottom who try to master the language of those on the top, which is English. The 'operational' staff are doing this in order to enhance their job opportunities within the school or outside. That is why I think that KIS has not made a big jump from Macaulay to a so-called multicultural community in India; it also shows that its efforts for "linguistic emancipation" are at a very low ebb.[18] The dominance of one language, English, is not automatically leading to multiculturalism, unless one understands multiculturalism as a way of life forced upon many who compromise for reasons of employment.

What is also missing at KIS are rigorous efforts to conceptualize multiculturalism in a social and historical perspective, for example, as a clear analysis of solidarity on the lines Aimé Césaire has suggested in his address to the First International Conference of Negro Writers and Artists as early as 1956. There, he distinguished between a "horizontal solidarity" and a "solidarity in time". By the first he meant a solidarity created by a special situation (in his case the colonial one imposed from without); by the second he understood a vertical solidarity which is due to the fact of an original unity (in his case of the African civilization).[19] So far KIS has neither analyzed its special situation nor its original unity. There is no question that Christianity as the original unity of the past is on the decline with the changing sociological complexion of the countries around and of the school, and has so far not been replaced by an alternative. The special situation which would demand a decolonization process and could thereby be a platform for solidarity is hardly understood or seen in this light by people in the school. Matters of daily utility clearly dominate matters of mind at KIS.

III

Earlier I have said that secularism could mean to deal with any number of faiths in an equal manner. But again I have to caution since we have to accept that this might be too difficult a proposal for a school of the nature and history of KIS. Man, over millenia and centuries of mental dependence on religion, has not become a multi-dimensional being in mind over night. Man is not truly living up to his intellectual potentialities but has often preferred to be guided by outside forces. Liberation was never a favourite word for many but, in turn, a threat to one's status of power, be they priest, teacher, or principal.

If this be the case, what then could be an alternative to a multi-dimensional secularism which still would deal with faiths? I should like to suggest a form of radical humanism which can transform individual and community life. Any system of thought has to embrace both, the individual and the group he lives in. If communism in the past neglected the diverse needs of the individual (not necessarily Marxism as a philosophy), then liberalism often neglects the community and its environment which shape the living conditions of the individual. Moreover, religions, though contemplating the interwoven cycle of individual and community, are shy of taking up, as a mass movement, the political problems which are to be faced while striving for a good and happy life for all. I am sure that humanism can provide such a framework. This form of humanism should, however, be a radical one, i.e., its strategy should be first in the interest of the person and not in the interest of a supernatural force. We know roughly what man is and what he needs, whereas we do not know what god is and needs. Humanism without this radical approach would be, at best, a mixture of idealistic, i.e., man and god-based rules and regulations which in the hands of a caste of priests would be vulnerable and probably be used against man in order to curb his individual freedom.[20]

A school like KIS could pursue this individual freedom as one of its major goals besides all the usual teaching and learning for academic excellence. The achievement of individual freedom is first freedom of thought. This is based on reason, a reason which helps distinguish between good and bad without the crutches of a super-structure, political or religious, and is the foundation of a self-sustained rational morality.[21] Let every pupil feel that he is being taken seriously in his development of thought. From a teacher's point of view there is no need of confusing this with laissez faire classroom management. Pupils do feel the advantage of being confronted with intellectual firmness and a framework of rules. Here I consider the flexibility of KIS a model, a boon which was probably brought about by its American shaped history. There is no doubt among educationists that the experiments of Americans in democratic education have formed modern pedagogy from the beginning of this century.

There remains the question of how to organize and administer a school which is secular, non-colonial, and striving for radical freedom and truth. First, it is not only the clash between professional and administrative authority, the conflict between the academician and the administrator in which the former fights for freedom and truth and the latter tries to 'fill slots' and to co-opt the former in order to exercise control and power.[22] It is more. It is the willingness to accept the primacy of educating over that of organizing, an age-old problem in education around the globe. If we can establish this primacy on all levels of work, then we might be able to review each and every problem from this point of view and not from an exterior one, then education might become productive and not only a function for an orderly creditation process. But as long as people in education "yearn for administrative status of some sort or other" and fall for "the illusions of power that go with administrative positions"[23] the realization of the primacy of educating is a goal too far away to be achieved.

Second, KIS has to solve conceptionally its biggest problem: to define what is meant by internationalism and multiculturalism in its four walls and beyond. To get this job done would mean to initiate a debate involving all. I think the reason for the failure so far is that people tend to think too much in terms of an institution which should function smoothly and too little in terms of eventually controversial values which should be examined in thorough discussions and which may perhaps change the institution. This constant exposure to conceptual change could be a fertile precondition for a dynamic understanding of multiculturalism.

In the present set-up of KIS, there is not much promise to enter this process of clarification soon since pre-conceived notions of living-together are dominating. Multiculturalism does not come about by Muslims and Hindus sharing a cup of tea or a common fast during Ramadan; and multiculturalism is not being practised while having pupils from several countries playing on the same soccer team. What we need is more. First, a *theory of education* for the type of school KIS is, i.e., a system of thought on education consisting of metaphysical speculations and value judgements supported by the results from empirical sociological and psychological research. Second, a *social theory* is needed which should "explain how the unintended consequences of our intentions and actions arise, and what kind of consequences arise if people do this or that or the other in a certain social situation".[24] A few emphatic ideas as in the school's two project designs of 1973 and 1994 are not a substitute for the work on these theories which should ultimately lead to a "reconnection of philosophy of education with social theory"[25] and would finally provide the ground for the conceptualization of multiculturalism. The whole conceptional deficit of the school demonstrates not a strength but a weakness because many of its problems, including the multicultural, are tied up with this deficit.

It makes a difference to educational philosophies and policies whether a school has a clear view of its hidden social theories. Whether they belong to 'individualism', 'functionalism', 'interactionism'[26] or whether they are a composite of these or others—to be forced to think about the order and functioning of a society will have its bearing on the selection of staff, the designs of syllabi, the formulation of educational goals, and also the working and living together of people in a school. Not to think about a school as part of the society in which it is located and the future society for which it educates, means to suffer from a deficit of focus and will finally neglect the full potential of the education one provides.

Let us now look at some ideas on multiculturalism which could eventually be taken up for discussion by a school like KIS.

Take, for example, M. Geyer who asserts that multiculturalism "explores the diversity and difference of cultural articulations and their *uneasy, embattled interactions*".[27] KIS, though professing to *multi*culturalism, does, according to Geyer's definition, in actual fact follow *mono*culturalism which "presumes a hierarchy of cultural values or a teleology of homogenizing progress emanating from a *single* center"[28] of, at KIS, Christianity. There are the occasional doubts at KIS, e.g., when the chairperson in an internal discussion paper points out "that we cannot...discuss multicultural educational programs safe within western walls",[29] but they have never been followed up in word or deed.[30] According to Geyer, multicultural education is not to put "clusters of particular and specialized knowledge of world regions and marginalized... constituencies into general education",[31] and it is not to insist "that enlightend Western values (liberty, individualism, property) have...become universal as the standard for global civilization",[32] but it is the beginning of a dissension how, e.g., "we can provide students with the appropriate tools of inquiry to mop the overflow of information about the world" and "how we can provide the knowledge to apprehend critically the fractured realities of the world before us in order to produce the knowledges...that allow us to transcend these fragments without destroying them individually while challenging the inequality and the violence of their interconnection".[33] The subjects of general education should, as to Geyer, qualify as multicultural education when they are :

(1) critical as opposed to instrumental or professional knowledge about global practices that network the world and their agents;

(2) the nondiscriminatory representation of the arrangements of individual and collective lives under the prevailing conditions of unsettlement or...global diasporas;

(3) the contestation of the definition of global common goods and the politics and the institutions that are associated with it; and

(4) the formulation of an epistemology and a pedagogy that facilitates the translation of local knowledge and their interconnection.[34]

One significant effort of multiculturalism in education would be to develop skills and knowledge which would facilitate the act of translation of each civilization to a recognition of each of them in their quality as shards. Geyer calls these skills and knowledge (following F. Jameson) "skills of transcoding" which 'are based on modes of inquiry that encompass...strategies of coping with the fear of otherness while honoring difference".[35]

Seeing the classroom as a civic space, we have to, however, accept the limits what a classroom can do. Is the analysis of power, as has been advocated above, really a form of violence that would split the mesh society of a multicultural class apart at their many seams? Or is the classroom the safe space for experimental thinking, involving encounters with the Other, with 'difference', and with theory? The Chicago Cultural Studies Group which has been discussing a critical multiculturalism for the past decade sees the limits of a classroom as follows:

> (T)he conventional logic of the classroom is such that the introduction of multiculturalism can be seen as an opportunity to recultivate pluralist consensus, while concern for critical thinking can be reduced to a fitness program in competence for future citizens. The classroom, moreover, is neither a typical public nor a place ideally capable of furnishing a heightened self-reflection that other public areas lack. Both the criticisms of the right and the aspirations of the left overestimate the transposability of criticism from the classroom to other contexts.[36]

Maybe all the activities to make a classroom more multicultural do really follow an illusion. Perhaps we should go back to a fundamental aim of education, viz. to enable pupils to understand themselves. This could result in both the acknowledgement of cultural identity and the inculcation of cultural values in them by, at the same time, avoiding to make one's own culture include all other cultures or to make other cultures subservient to one's own culture. Such an enlarged canon could benefit members of a majority as well as members of a minority, thinks Susan Mendus:

> 1. ...if we enlarge the canon and deploy it as a means of increasing self-understanding among the majority as well as the minority, one result may be that the majority will revise their own education of themselves.
>
> 2. ...by enlarging the canon we may come to see that some problems which are presented as problems of toleration are in fact problems of *recognition*.[37]

Let us finally reflect on the situation of a radical humanist teacher in such a scenario which is at the same time challenging and rewarding. It is challenging because a 'Christian multicultural' environment poses the problem whether the two can go together and how a radical humanist's commitment to the plurality of truth could be reconciled with the underlying mission of the institution. It is rewarding because a radical humanist will get first hand insight into the sociology of an organization with all its dynamic efforts and intelligent stalling to survive decently. To work in such a scenario is a chance to test the radical humanist axiology of freedom, knowledge and truth. Such an opportunity is certainly an eye-opener to how much of openness and critical analysis an institution is willing to grant its staff and how far a radical humanist can go in influencing the direction of the institution towards dealing with conflict in an unbiased manner, equality of cultures and religions, a variety of curricula and pedagogies, various forms of governance, and critical reflection on the effects of globalization in everyone's life.

Withstanding the pressure of a one-truth approach and defending one's position cannot be the sole strategies and purposes of a radical humanist teacher in such a scenario. This would be too passive, and passive resistance is certainly different from civil disobedience as Gandhi has aptly proved more than half a century ago. A radical humanist teacher wants to see some of his ideas and issues being discussed and eventually initiated into practice. They could be :

- the promotion of an understanding of different explanations of the existence of the world,
- the contribution to international solidarity with human suffering regardless of religious or communal affiliations (for this a sociological theory with the guiding principle of intervention to relieve this suffering would be helpful), and
- the assistance in rectifying fundamentalist attitudes.

In order to work for these objectives, the initial challenge to the radical humanist teacher is to overcome a boycott-only mentality which he may have developed in order not to be drawn into the net of the 'family'. Once this has been done, he has to set up dialogues and discussions with as many people as possible, both staff and pupils. This is a tedious process and should never only be confined to classes, organized meetings and seminars. These talks should be sought at many (work) places and whenever time permits. Ultimately these talks may help create more genuine openness in the intellectual and social realms of the institution which in turn may become a platform for changes in attitudes. Needless to say that this informal educative process needs a lot of stamina and perseverance from the teacher, and that results cannot be expected overnight.

There is also the danger that the radical humanist teacher becomes as dogmatic as any other believer in a faith. To prevent this I should like to suggest not to adhere to the ideas of one person only, be he Jesus, Buddha, Krishna, Marx, Gandhi or Roy, for the simple reason that such a mental *guru-shishya* relationship would be the first step in losing one's freedom, critical consciousness and independence of thought. Labels bind as much as they imprison. The radical humanist axiology may be strong enough to avoid the pitfalls of such a relationship, but this is no guarantee. Consequently, the radical humanist teacher in any institution would have to be radically critical first and foremost to himself.

There is no question that non-secular educational institutions have not only the right to exist and flourish but that they also deserve much support for some of their excellent academic work. To argue and oppose some of their basic tenets, e.g., in the case of KIS that a Christian identity should not be interpreted culturally and that "Christianity in itself is not a culture but...a set of beliefs that stands apart and judges all cultures"[38], does not mean to belittle such an institution and its goals. It is not a threat either but a signal to the institution that it is, intellectually and socially, taken seriously. After all, it would be humankind's loss if human beings were not able to live together in all their diversities. Preconditions of such a living together in a KIS-like situation would be :

- not to be infatuated with the absolute,
- to accept truth diversity as a fact, empirical reality, and as history,
- to attempt to understand this diversity cognitively,
- to continuously confront this diversity with one's own system of morality or spiritual existence and experience, which in turn would lead,
- to promote the 'relative' as resistance to authority.

Of these, the last two preconditions are the most crucial and difficult ones since it is in confrontation that we have to prove that critical thought and tolerance achieve a balance. Institutions like KIS and their members would have to practise this in their daily routines and dealings with dissent and recognition and, thus, make good education and multiculturalism in good education possible.[39]

References

1. J.J. Smolicz, 1981, p. 21.
2. Kodaikanal International School (ed.), 1995, pp. 4-6.
3. When I use the term 'structure', I shall employ it in the Chomskyan distinction of a "deep structure" as against the "surface structure". The first is paying as much reference as necessary to the abstract and, often, hidden meaning of an appearance and is compelling us to look beyond that what is seen and heard; by this we are dealing with the Why of an appearance and are accepting structures as products of thought. See to this chapter 10 "The Philosophy of Language and Mind" (pp. 125-38) in John Lyons, 1985.
4. Bertrand Russell, 1957, p. 31.
5. See to this the *Chairperson's Report to the Board of Management* (of Kodaikanal International School), September 25, 1995 (mimeographed), p. 2: "...we have to remain vigilant to ensure that we do not lose our important differences, those principles that make Kodai School what it is: our Christian heritage, the essential 'soul' of the school, the loving and *caring*, the respect for the individual." (emphasis mine)
6. M.N. Roy (1982, p. 149) explains this, with regard to religion, as a social necessity; as all other social phenomena, religion is not based upon "any eternal, immutable and absolute truths".
7. Spinoza, 1959, p. 77.
8. *Ibid.*, pp. 76-77.
9. Philip Spratt/M.N. Roy, 1986, p. 31. See to this also Bertrand Russell's (1984, p. 91) stimulating view on the value of philosophy which is to be found largely in its very uncertainty: "Philosophy, though unable to tell us with certainty what is the true answer to the doubts which it raises, is able to suggest many possibilities which enlarge our thoughts and free them from the tyranny as of custom. Thus, while diminishing our feeling of certainty as to what things are, it

greatly increases our knowledge as to what they may be; it removes the somewhat arrogant dogmatism of those who have never travelled into the region of liberating doubt, and it keeps alive our sense of wonder by showing familiar things in an unfamiliar aspect."

10. An example of inequality at KIS was, some years back, the struggle which had to be fought in order to get a Yoga course approved in the respective committee with the smallest possible margin of one vote. A strong group in this committee thought that Yoga was not an appropriate subject in a Christian-multicultural school regardless of its location.

11. See to this muddle Kodaikanal International School (ed.), 1995, pp. 4-5: "The school will acknowledge Jesus Christ and his teachings to be the foundation stone for achieving *all* its objectives." Amongst "all" are objectives as diverse as to "provide a creative, high quality, *academic* programme" and to "encourage the spiritual development of *each* member". (emphasis mine)

12. See to this the remarkable experience of a Quaker School in the U.S.A. about which Carolyn R. O'Grady (1992) reports in a frank article. Despite their strong Quaker spirituality, the school tried to change into an 'actively' multicultural school by seeking pupils "from a diverse range of family structures and racial, cultural, socio-economic and religious backgrounds " (p. 49). They found out, amongst other things, that they had to realize where people were "at different stages on the continuum of White racism awareness" (p. 54).

13. I should like to call these worldwide endeavours the traditional striving for international understanding in which the 'world citizen' has a lot of "concern for international issues" (Kodaikanal International School, ed.,[2] 1993, p. 7) and believes "in the innate good nature of human beings" (Jaganath Mohanty, 1988, p. 293) or works for "international educational cooperation" or "international educational relations" (William W. Brickman, 1956, p. 618).

14. Paulo Freire, 1970, pp. 121-135.

15. Bernhard S. Cohn, 1977, pp. 90-113.

16. Bruno Wambi, 1988, pp. 26-30.

17. Cf. Saral Jhingran, 1989, who besides lauding the Indian social structure "which is based on the firm foundation of a harmonious family life" (p. 107), also points out that the ideals of righteousness (*dharma*), social harmony and justice "are permanently vitiated by its basic assumption of the inequality of men" because of the division of society into classes and castes (p.108).

18. A.P. Rao, 1983, p. 12. J.J. Smolicz (1981) has this to say about the significance of language in a multicultural society: In such a society, the recognition of, for example, English as a lingua franca is usually not questioned, but "the acceptance of English by all ethnic groups must be taken as conditional on the understanding that, for those who wish to preserve their mother tongue, English represents an additional language rather than the sole and unique means of communication". (p. 22) The loss of the native tongue for a language-centred culture would herald a "cultural shift to the periphery. Ethnicity may still be maintained by appeal to the group's folk-lore, the preservation of family coherence and in-group marriage. When such a shift occurs however, the intellectual aspects of culture evaporate. In these circumstances, the cultural transmission chain tends to weaken in later generations. What is more, in its residual form, an ethnic culture is not very effective in interacting with the majority culture, at any other than domestic and folk levels. Significant cultural interaction can never occur on terms of equality, and the remaining pockets of ethnicity merely sustain structural division. It is when cultures have been reduced to such residues that they come to be associated with other variables like social class, religion or some other life-styles". (p. 25) I am afraid that KIS is part and parcel of such a process without realizing it.
19. Aimé Césaire, 1965, p. 149.
20. Cf. Reinhold Niebuhr, 1960, p . 6: "Even religious communities, if they are sufficiently large, and if they deal with issues regarded as vital by their members, resort to coercion to preserve their unity. Religious organizations have usually availed themselves of a convert type of coercion (excommunication and interdict) or they have called upon the police power of the state."
21. Contrary to what many admirers in the West think about the 'spiritual' ancient India, there was also another side, viz. a system of education which was strictly patterned on critical and rational learning and invited the student to take nothing for granted and to question each and everything. The two texts which document this clearly are the *Tantra-yukti* and the *Nyayasutra*. See to this Radha Kumal Mookerji, 1974, pp. 317-18.
22. Philip C. Schlechty, 1976, p. 209: "Sometimes the system handles threats by experienced teachers by co-opting the teacher" by, for example, promoting him to a supervisory function, "ostensibly so that he may inspire others. The effect may be, however, that the burden of administrative work and the requirements of the new role will remove a vital grass roots source of change".

23. V.V. John, 1978, pp. x, ix.
24. Karl R. Popper, 1972, p. 125.
25. Ruth Jonathan, 1995, p. 94.
26. See to this Barry Barnes, 1995, pp. 11, 37, 71.
27. Michael Geyer, 1993, p. 501 (emphasis mine)
28. *Ibid.*, p. 501 (emphasis mine)
29. *Chair's Report to the Board of Management* (of Kodaikanal International School), April 1995, p. 2.
30. This is not to say that KIS does not make an effort to address the multicultural problem; it only asserts that it does so in order to achieve a harmonious veneer without going to the roots of differences or similarities. See to this two examples from different activities: first the 'moving' case of a day of sharing between KIS elementary school with an elementary school from the same area ("Elementary School Reaches Out to Reaching the Unreached", *KIS Newsletter*, Vol. 3, no. 4, April 1998, p. 15); the other the results of an (American) questionnaire answered by 101 of the staff as an exercise for the school's accreditation to an American accreditation agency: on a scale of 0 to 5, 3.79 was the positive average for the statement, "The curriculum provides for the development of the skills and understanding necessary to function in a global society", and 3.63 for "The curriculum is free of cultural and gender biases" (*Complete results of the questionnaire*, January 10, 1997, p. 96, mimeographed). I do not want to comment on the rightness and relevance of these figures but only to point out that questions like these are being included in the discussion at school, albeit only in a peripheral manner.
31. M. Geyer, 1993, p. 515.
32. *Ibid.*, p. 524.
33. *Ibid.*, p. 527.
34. *Ibid.*, p. 528.
35. *Ibid.*, p. 531. One could go even a step further and claim that "Multiculturalism Does Not Exist" as Stanley Fish (1997, p. 378) does. He argues that "boutique multiculturalism" is always to "stop short of approving other cultures at a point where some value at their centre generates an act that offends against the canons of civilized decency as they have been either declared or assumed." (p. 378) And even "strong multiculturalism", though it "will want to accord a deep

respect to all cultures at their core" (p. 382) is not in a very distinct position "but a somewhat deeper instance of the shallow category of boutique multiculturalism" because the strong multiculturalist finally uses "some supra-cultural universal" hidden up his sleeve from the very beginning when he faces the dilemma to, for example, tolerate Khomeni's call for the death of S. Rushdie or to condemn "the core intolerance of that culture" (p. 383).

36. Chicago Cultural Studies Groups 1992, p. 547.
37. Susan Mendus, 1995, pp. 199-200. (emphasis mine)
38. Kodaikanal International School (ed.), 1995, p. 3.
39. The material of this appendix has been drawn and expanded from two earlier publications see Bernd Pflug, 1992 and 1997.

9

The Intercultural and Humanist Rationale of a History of Ideas Curriculum

I

Teaching ideas at the end of the 20th century has to be taken up against the backdrop of two factors which have, above all others, shaped human history of this century of extremes. The great historian of ideas Isaiah Berlin opens his essay, "The Pursuit of the Ideal" with these two phenomena:

> One is the development of the natural sciences and technology, certainly the greatest success story of our time—to this great and mounting attention has been paid from all quarters. The other...consists in the great ideological storms that have altered the lives of virtually all mankind: the Russian Revolution and its aftermath—totalitarian tyrannies of both right and left and the explosions of nationalism, racism and, in places, religious bigotry which, interestingly enough, not one among the most perceptive social thinkers of the nineteenth century had ever predicted.[1]

Berlin continues that these characteristics of the 20th century are "the most demanding of explanation and analysis", but that we should well realize that they have begun with ideas in the minds of people:

> ideas about what relations between men have been, are, might be and should be; ...how they came to be transformed in the name of a vision of some supreme goal in the minds of the leaders, above all of the prophets with armies at their backs. Such ideas are the substance of ethics.

Ethical thought consists of the systematic examination of the relations of human beings to each other, the conceptions, interests and ideals from which human ways of treating one another spring, and the systems of value on which such ends of life are based. These beliefs about how life should be lived, what men and women should be and do, are objects of moral inquiry; and when applied to groups and nations, and, indeed, mankind as a whole, are called political philosophy, which is but ethics applied to society.[2]

The present course in History of Ideas is an endeavour in moral and political philosophy in this Berlinan sense.

India is part of the 20th century shaped by the natural sciences and revolutions. She has had her share of inventions in science and technology and has experienced painful aftermaths in politics and fundamentalist movements. She has experimented with prophets, armies, relations between men, and various kinds of ethical thought. A course in the history of ideas has to take into account both the international as well as the national scenarios concerning the two factors of shape. Ideas cannot be taught in a social and cultural vacuum. And since the students in this course are mainly from South Asia, moral and political questions, problems and examples will have to come from a similar experiential background. However, answers do not always arise from the same background but also from far away shores of thought and sentiments. Borders need not be regarded as eternal barriers. Here we have to face tension while planning course, aims and content: the near vs. the far, the familiar vs. the strange, the known vs. the unknown. This means the aim of such a course cannot be the harmonious solution to a problem at any cost; rather, it may be a struggle with contrasting views and actions. In such a struggle, students will be confronted with viewpoints they have never heard before, viewpoints which hurt when they do not match their own, viewpoints which they would like to reject summarily were it not for the educational situation. The intention is to address the deep-seated feeling that everything outside one's own horizon is considered alien, not useful, and even dangerous. Despite an unprecedented increase in international contacts, travelling and migration, the instinct to feel well only within one's own herd is still strong particularly among middle class students. I should like to classify this aim as *existential* in the sense that it goes deep to the 'heart' of the human predicament to go beyond mental, social and cultural boundaries. It would help students demystify their own backgrounds, conditionings, and prejudices.

A second, more traditional aim of this course is to be achieved in the realm of the *cognitive* and covers what we usually call 'thinking'. Here we have to distinguish with John Dewey between the active, vital, dynamic and exciting process of thinking that is constantly testing hypotheses from the end of this process which is thought. Thought is generally the fruit and termination of thinking, but it may also be the beginning of thinking, namely, of a new chain of producing thought.[3] Thus it is at the same time ends and results, ends representing the completion of something, results representing something that is never complete and a stage achieved in some continuous inquiry.[4] And this is precisely what is hoped to be accomplished in this course: a continuous process of thinking resulting in one's own conclusion while working with some selected ideas of humankind. By this we also make it a point to offer this course in the sense that it *is* life and not only preparation *for* life as so much of even higher education is being considered. Teacher and students are expected to use all their intellectual energies for this important task. In this enterprise the intellectual lives of those involved are more important than the full competition of a canon of topics.

With these aims, the existential and the cognitive, we have taken a conscious decision against a historiography of ideas course, but have opted for an *exemplary* approach as to ideas and their sources.[5] We have decided for creativity at the expense of comprehensive history. In sum, we are to adhere to the primacy of thinking. John Dewey, in his famous book, *How We Think*, published in 1910, has offered a five-stage scheme for what he called "the complete act of thought". Though it would be rather stifling to follow its stages faithfully and meticuously in each and every lesson (as it would be with Herbart's stages), its guiding value can be of immense help for a course like ours. Dewey's stages are:

(i) a felt difficulty;

(ii) its location and definition;

(iii) suggestion of a possible solution;

(iv) development by reasoning of the bearings of the suggestion;

(v) further observation and experiment leading to its acceptance or rejection; that is, the conclusion of belief or disbelief.[6]

It is but obvious that students should be informed about these two fundamental aims of this course before they decide to opt for it or not. The same applies to an outline of course content and methodology. Unfortunately, this practice is hardly used in Indian higher education. Participation of learners begins with their decision about what they want to learn and what they do not want to learn. It is to be noted that for this course further objectives which would go into details of individual lessons seem to be superfluous since they would limit the creativity of a teacher and his students to make each lesson an exercise of existential and intellectual discovery. A curricular framework as described in this paper is usually enough for a good teacher and a group of motivated students to work successfully for their own intellectual and moral betterment.

II

Both these aims of the course, the existential and cognitive, are reflected in the basic rationale of its curriculum: the *intercultural* and the *humanist*. A philosophical foundation is a must for every curriculum work because it tells us and others something about our understanding of life, the intentions we have concerning education, and whether recipients of education can, eventually, trust the, hopefully, congruent nature of a programme. This congruent nature should consist of a consonance of theory and practice which means for our course: if existence and thinking are the overriding aims, then an appropriate way of putting them into practice has to be developed, then the teaching has to be 'existential' and 'thinking'.

In describing the intercultural element of the rationale of the course, we are following largely one of today's most original thinkers in this area of thought, Raimon Panikkar.[7] In his view, 'culture' can be pursued in two ways, (a) as a field that makes it possible for us to cultivate the world, and (b) as the specific form of human nature. In both these assertions we are dealing with logos and mythos and can, consequently, not operate with cultural universals, meaningful concrete contents valid for all cultures and for humankind throughout all times. At this stage, interculturality steps in and is meant to play a major role, so to speak the "philosophical imperative of our times", answering the twofold temptation of monoculturalism and multiculturalism.[8]

Panikkar considers monoculturalism "lethal" because it "asphyxiates other cultures through oppression".[9] His argument runs as follows: monoculturalism is "subtle" and "well-intentioned" because it "consists in admitting a vast range of cultural diversity but against the unique backdrop of a common denominator",[10] which could be scientific concepts, the law of causality or translating phenomena of nature into algebraic terms. Modern man would not be doubting scientific progress to accept cultural relativism. His evolutionary thinking, his linear conception of time, and his vision that humankind and human life consist in "developing", would give him always enough arguments to theoretically justify monoculturalism.[11] Even a pluricultural attitude would not be a consolation since only "one culture sets the rule of the game" which other cultures would have to follow suit.[12]

The other extreme opposite is multiculturalism which would lead to a "war of cultures" or would condemn us to "cultural apartheid" which in the long run would become very stifling.[13] Panikkar thinks that multiculturalism can never be achieved because of the primordial function of each culture "which consists in offering a vision of reality which allows man to live his life". He confirms the possibility of the existence of a plurality of cultures without mutual connection but obviously not the *co*existence of their fundamental diversity in today's world.[14] Panikkar does not deny that "there can be a transcultural validity of certain formal ways of thinking", but we must not forget "that every universitality is formal and that formality presupposes certain axioms (precisely formal ones) that are postulated or acknowledged".[15] Moreover, he admits that the dominant culture today, technocracy, has made multiculturalism de facto impossible: "Technocracy...has practically penetrated the four directions of the earth. We may have to surmount to dominate it, but we cannot ignore its ubiquity.

Maybe it is destined to become the unique culture which will replace all others; but this does not mean that it is a super-culture encompassing all others."[16]

The way out for Panikkar is to seek a middle way: interculturality and its process of interculturalization.[17] He maintains that the cultural relativity of an intercultural discourse has nothing to do with cultural relativism since the "relativity inherent to interculturality does not question the discoveries of a culture, but neither does it absolutize them". Rather it relativizes them, i.e., "it considers them valid and legitimate within a given culture and within the parameters admitted by the latter; in a word: within the encompassing myth of that culture".[18] Even if cultures are mutually incompatible, we cannot insist that they are incommunicable. No culture would remain static without destroying itself; that is why no culture would be, at least implicitly, without interculturality, and so would be no human being. "All cultures are the result of a continuous mutual fecundation." This also rules out the existence of one unique culture; it would be "as incomprehensible and impossible as a single universal language and as one man alone".[19] Panikkar concludes that interculturality is the complete form of human culture.[20]

For our curriculum in the History of Ideas we shall be guided first and foremost by interculturality both in content and method. The selected content shall contain sufficient intercultural matter, and the ways of working with this matter should be largely "radically critical of the intercultural enterprise itself". Robert Vachon has listed three main methods:

Contrasting

> To contrast is not to compare; pluralism and interculturalism (are) not preoccupied with multiplicity or diversity as such, but with the incommensurability of human constructions with regard to the subject of homologous questions.

Imparative

> The approach is not comparative but imparative (from medieval Latin: *imparare*, to learn), i.e., an open philosophical

attitude, ready to *learn from* other cultures/philosophies of the world, without pretending to compare them from an objective neutral, transcendent point of view. It is a matter of being ready to undergo the philosophical experience of other peoples, of being constitutively ready to question the very foundations (the unconscious pre-suppositions) of one's own culture, without ever leaving the latter.

Dialogical

It is a dialogical approach, i.e., open not only to dialectical confrontation and to a rational dialogue with another culture, but to a dialogue which goes *beyond logos*, and where the meeting takes place at the level of the *mythos*...Moreover, it is an approach which seeks to form its philosophical vision of the world by systematically taking into consideration the whole of the human experience inasmuch as this is possible in a concrete situation.[21]

It goes without saying that to realize these three ways in day-to-day classes is to rely on dedicated teaching and learning as a mutual act between teacher and students.

A second, equally important, essential for the rationale of our curriculum is the humanist aspect. As in the case of the intercultural, many forms of humanism have been traded in the academic community over centuries, from a religious and spiritual humanism as in the cases of, e.g., Gandhi and Radhakrishnan[22] to any number of scientific kinds of humanism. To contrast the religious/metaphysical line of argumentation of R. Panikkar in his conception of the intercultural, and to practise in this the first radical way of interculturalism postulated by Vachon, we deem it appropriate and helpful to refer to a radically anthropocentric form of humanism in the form of M.N. Roy's radical humanism which he developed in the years between 1948 and 1954.[23] We surely do not think that the curriculum should be understood and taught solely from one philosophical or ideological vantage point, on the other hand, we do not advocate that a process of clarification of values and beliefs (that is what students and teacher practically do in such a course) can and should be done in a vacuum with no shoulders to rub and no issues to fight about. Radical humanism will provide plenty of food for thought and argument; one of the reasons would be that it simply rejects the equality of logos and mythos which we have met in R. Panikkar's conception of interculturality. We have selected radical humanism, however, not primarily for its didactic function in producing a counterweight to R. Panikkar's interculturality, but for its worthiness as an alternative.

There is another reason for following the humanist way of thought. To teach in the History of Ideas is to work in a perfect environment while dealing with humanism in its broadest sense. It provides an ideal opportunity to address the quest of humankind to find explanations of life. To teach this to young adults is to work with people who are still enthusiastic and malleable enough to accept new horizons; on the other hand, they are mature enough to relate some of their own experiences to the theoretical discussions in class.

M.N. Roy's exposition of radical humanism runs as follows: Human sovereignty is best guaranteed and promoted by a philosophy which can be called "physical realism". It is a philosophy that accepts conceptual thought *and* scientific method not as two different things: "Conceptual thought is generalization of an abstraction from experience. Scientific thinking is stimulated by empirical knowledge, and is also informed and guided by man's conceptual equipments."[24] The universe and the human being are physical systems, the former being law-governed, the latter being able to choose. Between the two lies the world of biological evolution. Reason which results from the consciousness of man being an integral part of the law-governed universe harmonizes the two.[25]

Man is essentially rational, asserts Roy. This innate rationality is the "only guarantee" of a morality which is an appeal to conscience. This is nothing mystic or mysterious but a biological function and thus the foundation of a harmonious social order which is also a moral order.[26]

The supreme value of life is freedom because "the urge for freedom is the essence of human existence" and can be traced all the way down the biological evolution; this tempts Roy to claim all human morality as evolutionary (without giving convincing

evidence).[27] Since man's struggle for survival is eternal, he will never conquer the universe and his urge for freedom is, therefore, also undying, eternal. In this struggle for freedom "man discovers truth" which "is neither a mystic-metaphysical category nor an abstract value" but the content of man's knowledge. Out of this Roy deduces that the hierarchy of the humanist axiology is "freedom, knowledge, truth". These three are not autonomous but interrelated, "logically as well as ontologically".[28]

Roy considers this radical or new humanism primarily a social philosophy, embedded in a general philosophy of nature, namely, physical realism, which traces emotion and intelligence, will and reason to their common biological origin, and, thus, "reconciles the romantic doctrine of revolution, that man makes history, with the rationalist notion of orderly social progress", revolution being understood as an "acceleration in the tempo of the evolutionary process".[29]

In the anti-Marxist turn of his later years, Roy finally concludes that ideas can hardly be referred to economic incentives but are formed in the mind of man and exist by themselves; no causal relation could be traced "between social events and movements of ideas". That is why he calls ideation a "psychological process".[30]

Though revolution is the aim, it has to be a revolution which "must go beyond an economic reorganization of society" and which has to address man as a thinking being in a cosmopolitan commonwealth. For this purpose, Roy demands forcefully that the "education of the citizen" is accepted as a condition to create a society which is "conducive to common progress and prosperity without encroaching on the freedom of the individual."[31]

This rather rigorous, at times even dogmatic, worldview must not be imposed on students as the only possible explanation of man and the universe; this would totally contradict our aim of 'thinking'. It is one amongst other models of explanation. But it serves as a suitable counterthought to the rather vague conceptualization of interculturality by R. Panikkar. So what is its concrete impact on a curriculum in the History of Ideas? There are three factors which can be drawn from a radical humanist approach and used in the course:

(a) A radical humanist approach is never expecting people to simply believe in the pronouncements of any authority. It invites questioning and critical thought and puts the independently thinking man at the centre of the activity to understand himself and the world. Whatever is taught, including the content of this present course, should be doubted first, examined critically, and then refuted or eventually integrated in one's own system of knowledge, beliefs, and values.

(b) This is only possible when man does not feel dependent on any form of supreme being. The mysterious has to be cancelled as a guiding agency. The physical has to take precedence over the metaphysical as a point of reference. The idea of God has to be discussed but should not be made the overriding and decision-making instance. But even this must not be imposed on students of a course which is taught in a radical humanist way.

(c) The radical humanist approach should develop in human beings a deep respect for other human beings. The nature of man is considered essential inasmuch as it makes man not a living machine but a thinking and feeling being. A curriculum in the History of Ideas must, therefore, never neglect the needs, desires, compulsions and limitations of its students. Drawing upon the history of thought, even if only on selected thought, should help students become clearer about their own nature, how it has become, and how it can be used for one's own fulfillment and that of society.

Both the intercultural and the humanist as outlined above will help us in deciding epistemological considerations, viz. how we can select, from the range of human knowledge, what to teach and in which sequence. The intercultural will force us to accept a broad range of selection, not restricting it to content from one culture only, but also not falling prey to the temptation of a mere pluricultural selection. The humanist will make us aware of how radically we can see man as the centre of all thoughts and things. But despite its compactness of argument and conviction, it will offer plenty of opportunities to discuss this anthropocentrism critically and to disagree with its presuppositions and conclusions.

This will make us careful in selecting content which is of dogmatic character. Rather we attempt to find a balance which is signified by openness, strength, and clear-sightedness.

It goes without saying that the topics and texts selected for this curriculum (see part IV) have to be understood as exemplary and tentative matter. The 15 ideas and their texts could be easily replaced by several sets of 15 different ideas and texts which would make the same, if not more, sense. Selections of topics and sources are never finished for a curriculum in the History of Ideas, particularly not when its essential intention is pedagogical and not scholarly; selection and replacement are ongoing; and a canon must never become static. If it does, it will lose its tempting and exciting character and become self-defeating in its fundamental aim of the existential and cognitive development of students or, for that matter, anyone who would involve himself with the evolution of ideas in human history.

III

The topics of the curriculum should be only used as introductory and guiding matter of a whole complex of ideas. Out of this follows that the central ideas should be taught concentric and not strictly linear. The discussion of a problem presented by an idea would be as important as the information about the idea. Practically it would mean to explain and to understand a gamut of ideas with the help of a few pages of major original texts each of which would stimulate the discussion of a variety of problems. That is why our approach is selective rather than comprehensive and integrative rather than chronological (though the question of historical context must not be neglected). It is hoped that such an approach will enable students to understand and assess the mesh of ideas which have contributed to their own being and becoming.

Five realms have been identified for explanation and understanding of the content matter. They should be considered while we teach and learn albeit not rigidly in the given sequence and not always with an equal distribution among the five. Several of the topics demand a focus on two or three of these realms only, others just on one, and probably only a few are suitable for a covering of all the five realms, which are:

1. the *historical* which examines the process how an idea has evolved out of an earlier idea in a given society in its historical context,
2. the *socio-economic* which investigates the emergence of an idea in a given society in its historical-political context;
3. the epistemological which analyses the nature of knowledge embodied in an idea,
4. the *existential* which discusses the relevance of an idea to today's lifeworld; and
5. the *intercultural* which anticipates the significance of an idea in a 'multicultural' society.

The 'existential' and the 'intercultural of these realms are distinctively different from the same categories elucidated above as to the rationale of the curriculum. Amongst the realms they are treated as academic departments; as fundamentals of the rationale they constitute a whole 'atmosphere' of the total 'project curriculum'.

At this stage we have to think about method, i.e., how to teach in this curriculum. One of the great models of teaching has always been the Socratic (another being Uddalaka's in the *Upanishads* — unfortunately and perhaps undeservedly less popular than the Socratic in general education), and we do regard the Socratic very appropriate for a course in the History of Ideas. Let us summarize this system of teaching and learning along the lines of Paul Woodruff's excellent exposition.[32]

He begins with the most significant feature of Socratic education, viz. to put the responsibility for learning on the learner, and categorizes Socratic education into three salient features: critical and consistent thinking, teacherless education, and the hope that education transforms people's lives for the better.[33] In Socratic conversations, self-education is the main aim, and the main rule is to say only what one believes when one is questioned.[34] Learners are responsible for their answers, not teachers: "The pedagogical justification for such teaching seems clear: learners are more likely to take a lesson to heart if they feel that it belongs to them and was theirs from the beginning."[35] Woodruff describes the procedure in eight points:

1. The teacher denies he is a teacher and takes the attitude of a learner.
2. Lectures by the teacher are rare and, if given, the teacher is not responsible for their content.
3. Questions from the teacher to the learner are the main form of communication.
4. The learner is responsible for any answer.
5. Questions may aim at answers which would be evidence to support knowledge claims of the learner.
6. Usually with the consent of the learner, the teacher introduces standards for knowledge.
7. The teacher subscribes to positive statements of beliefs which have been elicited by questions.
8. Consistency demands that the learner therefore rejects an earlier statement.[36]

In an incisive judgement, Woodruff then argues (and shattering on his way many myths so dear to liberal teachers) that today's popular open-question teaching is *not* Socratic because it teaches to accept each other's ideas, to follow each other's intellectual leads with respect, to impose no rule but an open mind, and does not control the evaluation of answers.[37] Socratic teaching would reject this as a rudderless enterprise. Indeed, Socratic education means to be thoroughly in control of the method. And even 'teacherless education' is not without an ideal teacher though Socrates is convinced "that he does not know enough to be a teacher as he understands what that is".[38] His true teacher should have both the authority of a practitioner who knows his craft or profession (techné) and the articulate wisdom of a sage "who gives answers to questions, but these answers may be enigmatic or at least challenging to the questioner". Besides this, the sage may choose "not to answer at all, to be a silent teacher".[39]

This kind of teaching and learning can be realized only, if a teacher believes, with Socrates, "that human beings generally have sufficient resources to take responsibility for learning".[40] Truly a humanist demand! To try to teach in a Socratic-like manner would mean to try to be congruent: teaching great ideas is to accept a multitude of thought which have gone into these ideas over the past two to three millenia; in order to do justice to them and those who want to think critically about them, the Socratic method seems to leave much room for practice within a rigorous framework of quality in which the teacher will not let the learning get away with sloppy thinking or unsubstantiated knowledge claims.

IV

In this last section we reproduce two syllabi. The first one is the present one which has been taught by the author in the academic year 1997-98 at Kodaikanal Christian College and whose rationale has been expounded in this paper. The second one is of a course the author has taught in different circumstances as an "Introduction to Philosophy" and highlights the method of philosophizing which is also central to the rationale of the present course in the History of Ideas (and is therefore given here as an appendix).

Kodaikanal Christian College
History of Ideas
Syllabus

The main objective of this course in intercultural philosophy is to help students form a cosmopolitan and humanist sensibility which is simultaneously intellectual, moral and social. The course is taught in a combination of lectures, discussions and seminars over one semester with four class hours per week. Students are assessed on the basis of oral and written course work without a final examination. The course is divided into three themes—the metaphysical (nos. 1-4), the social (nos. 5-10) and the scientific (nos. 11-15):

0. Introduction to the rationale of the syllabus
   Interculturality—Panikkar: Religion, Philosophy and Culture Humanism—Roy: Reason, Romanticism and Revolution
1. Being and the Self
   Rigveda

Brihadaranyaka Upanishad

2. Central Harmony
   Confucius: The Analects
   Tiruvalluvar: The Kural
3. God
   Thomas Aquinas: Summa Theologiae
   Al Ghazali: The Revival of the Religious Sciences
4. Atheism
   Kumarila: Slokavartika
   Sartre: Existentialism is a Humanism
5. Duty
   Kant: Metaphysical Foundations of Morals
6. Rights
   Paine: Rights of Man
7. Freedom
   Mill: On Liberty
8. Historical Materialism
   Engels/Marx: The German Ideology
9. Welfare
   Gandhi: Sarvodaya
10. Feminism
    Beauvoir: The Second Sex
11. Evolution
    Darwin: The Origin of Species
12. Knowledge
    Russell: Human Knowledge
13. Science
    Einstein: Principles of Research
14. Cybernetics
    Wiener: The Human Use of Human Beings
15. Universe
    Hawking: A Brief History of Time

"Introduction to Philosophy"

In *philosophizing* we are on our own, and the ideas of others must not come into our way while perceiving, thinking and grappling with appearance, reality and transcendence. It is not that we can build in philosophy on accumulated knowledge in biology with knowledge which is either right or wrong; instead we have to start again and again with the basic and age-old questions which have troubled and challenged humankind ever since. There is no textbook-like short-cut to philosophic understanding. That is why the study of the history of philosophy is helpful only later when we are experienced in the technique of philosophizing.

On the other hand, we can certainly learn from what others have thought before, i.e., we are not exempted from reading the great authors. Through them we may gain an insight into the varieties of existential problems of humankind. They can open our eyes to what is not clear and what we want to make clearer for ourselves. This, of course, can threaten our normal life in its complacency and ritualistic behaviour. Those who do not like to be exposed to this, should not study philosophy.

But there is a satisfaction for those who try a deeper inquiry into philosophical problems. They may come up with the conviction that man is not only living in this world but that this world is also living in him. To cope with the first is comparatively easy and can lead to a progressive mastery of this world as our scientific and technological advances in recent times have shown. But to deal with the world in us, is a different story. Here our intellectual struggle begins from scratch in order to come to terms with our delusions. The world in us is as we are making the world in us and is thus not as objective as something we are confronted with in nature.

But one could insist, why should we understand the worked in us if we have never realized it so and are happy without it. If this be the case, then we should not touch philosophy and should continue the slumber of blissful ignorance. There is no harm in this. But if we are driven by the desire to question the world in us and to explore its design and mental map, then philosophizing is the right thing. It then may become the road to freedom, surely an endless one which might produce more pain and anguish than clarification. Whether we want to walk this road by stressing more the technical or by emphasizing more the meditative points of philosophizing, does not matter much, as long as we are radically trying to contribute to our own knowledge of the self.

Philosophizing is like watering or emptying an ocean. We will neither be able to add a significant amount of water to an ocean nor to empty it. But in order to get an idea of an ocean, we have to take a sip from it rather than to get it explained from outside. Let the sip be salty, for salty are the thoughts of philosophers; and should their thoughts taste like sugar, then they are false and want to seduce us into a state of self-righteousness. The salty ideas, however, can lead us to creative confusion which is a precondition for coming out on our own.

Studying the ideas of great thinkers (in their own words), means to deal with mortals though. They died as we have to die one day, and death is practically the only certainty we have as philosophic knowledge on life. Not so what is beyond it—which is for some already one of the prominent issues of philosophy, but the best of thinking has so far not been contributed much to its understanding.

Philosophizing may come up with the cultivation of a worldview but not necessarily so. Whether such a worldview is a necessity depends on one's mentality and outlook. Here the Indian tradition is more liberal than the Western where questions of style and technique prevail. But both agree on knowledge as always temporary in form and content, and those who tell us otherwise either believe in an ideology or a religion only.

The few texts I would use in this introductory course are:

Samkhaya-Sutra by Kapila

The Apology of Socrates by Plato

The Consolation of Philosphy by Boethius

The Critique of Practical Reason by Kant

The Subject as Freedom by K.C. Bhattacharyya

References

1. Isaiah Berlin, 1998, p. 1.
2. *Ibid.*, p. 1.
3. I.K. Davies, 1975, p. 305.
4. *Ibid.*, p. 303.
5. In this we are *not* following A.O. Lovejoy's conception of the historiography of ideas though he is, rightly and widely, accepted as the founder of the discipline 'History of Ideas'. The main reasons for not following his model is twofold: first, the present course is too short, and second, Lovejoy's understanding is more directed towards an academic, scholarly occupation with histories of ideas. Instead, the nature of our course is more signified by its pedagogical character to help students understand concepts of life through great ideas of humankind. For the record, however, here is a summary of A.O. Lovejoy's conception. He defined his understanding of the 'History of Ideas' in the preface to his *Essays in the History of Ideas* as follows: "It studies the presence and influence of the same ideas in very different provinces of thought and in different periods; thus, an idea that may have originated in logic may turn up in biology, or vice versa. (2) There are certain catchwords, such as 'nature' that have taken on new meanings over a period of time, although the people using them are seldom aware of their ambiguities. The historian of ideas will analyze these various meanings as they occur. (...) (3) It has also been noticed that a given author will prove susceptible to the emotional aura of certain terms and, probably because of this, will waver between a valid meaning of an idea and an incongruous meaning. It is usually assumed that the thought of a given writer must be consistent and unified; but by accepting this assumption, a historian may overlook precisely those thoughts expressed by a writer that were in fact influential." (Paul Edwards, (ed.) vol. 5, 1967, p. 96)
6. Quoted in Alan Ryan, 1998, p. 404.
7. Raimon Panikkar has elucidated the 'intercultural' in numerous publications on the interface of philosophy and theology; however, for our purpose it suffices to focus on one of his concise deliberations of recent times (Raimon Panikkar, 1998)
8. *Ibid.*, p. 110.
9. *Ibid.*, p. 113.
10. *Ibid.*, p. 110.

11. *Ibid.*, p. 111.
12. *Ibid.*, p. 112.
13. *Ibid.*, p. 113.
14. *Ibid.*, p. 112.
15. *Ibid.*, p. 112.
16. *Ibid.*, p. 113.
17. *Ibid.*, p. 113.
18. *Ibid.*, p. 111.
19. *Ibid.*, p. 113.
20. *Ibid.*, p. 114.
21. Robert Vachon, 1998, pp. 40-41.
22. See e.g. S. Radhakrishnan, 1992, p. 25.
23. It is interesting to note that Raimon Panikkar is one of the strongest opponents of any form of humanism. We are quoting here a full paragraph (R. Panikkar, 1973, pp. 78-79) to demonstrate this: "It is not by chance that the most characteristic crypto-heresy of the west since the Middle Ages has been and still is humanism. Of this the explanation is simple. One side humanism is a healthy reaction against an excessive emphasis on eschatology and a certain anti-natural supernaturalism. On the other, it cannot fail to be a temptation to mankind now arrived at the age of reflection, for it concentrates all human life and even religion on man and his anthropocentric perfection. Man cannot submit to the rule of egoism; the earth is not made up only of mountains; religion does not come in order to slay man but to save him. The staggering affirmation of Christian belief is just that it is virtually necessary to save not only the 'lofty' part of man, his soul, but the whole man including his body, indeed the whole cosmos. By stressing these truths lopsidedly, however, humanism very easily loses sight of the whole, upsets the balance and tends to become sheer naturalism." Radical humanism is called by M.N. Roy also "new humanism", see the last chapter in M.N. Roy, 1989, and M.N. Roy, 1981.
24. M. N.Roy, 1989, pp. 493-494.
25. *Ibid.*, pp. 495-496.
26. *Ibid.*, p. 496.
27. *Ibid.*, p. 496.
28. *Ibid.*, p. 497.

29. *Ibid.*, p. 498.
30. *Ibid.*, p. 498.
31. *Ibid.*, p. 499.
32. Paul Woodruff, 1998, pp. 14-31.
33. *Ibid.*, p. 14.
34. *Ibid.*, pp. 16, 18.
35. *Ibid.*, p. 19.
36. *Ibid.*, pp. 19, 20.
37. *Ibid.*, p. 21.
38. *Ibid.*, p. 22.
39. *Ibid.*, p. 26.
40. *Ibid.*, p. 22.

Bibliography

Adler, Mortimer J.: *Ten Philosophical Mistakes*, New York: Macmillan, 1985

Améry, Jean: *Radical Humanism*. Selected essays, edited and translated by Sidney Rosenfeld and Stella P. Rosenfeld, Bloomington: Indiana University Press, 1984

Appiah, Kwame Anthony: "Is the Post- in Postmodernism the Post- in Postcolonial?" *Critical Inquiry*, Vol. 17, no. 2, Winter 1991, pp. 336-357

Arendt, Hannah: *On Violence*, New York: Harcourt, Brace & World, 1970

Arendt, Hannah: *The Human Condition*, Chicago: The University of Chicago Press, 1989 (1958)

Arnowitz, Standley: "Mass Culture and the Eclipse of Reason: The Implications for Pedagogy" *College English*, Vol. 38, no. 8, 1977, pp. 768-774

Banerjee, Archana: *Models of Metaphilosophy*, Calcutta: Minerva, 1989

Banerjee, Nikunja Vihari: *Concerning Human Understanding*. Essays on the Common-sense Background of Philosophy, London: Allen & Unwin, 1958

Baran, Gary L.: A Buddhist and Hindu Critique of Descartes, in: Ninian Smart/B. Srinivasa Murthy (eds.): *East-West Encounters in Philosophy and Religion*, Mumbai: Popular Prakashan, 1996, pp. 245-253

Bernstein, J.M.: *Recovering Ethical Life*, Jurgen Habermas and the future of critical theory, London: Routledge, 1995

Bernstein Richard J.: *Habermas and Modernity*, Cambridge: Polity Press, 1985

Bhaba Homi K.: *The Location of Culture*, London: Routledge, 1995 (1994)

Bhattacharya, Gopinath: *Essays in Analytical Philosophy*, Calcutta: Sanskrit Pustak Bhandar, 1989

Blake, Nigel: "Modernity and the Problem of Cultural Pluralism" *Journal of Philosophy of Education*, Vol. 26, no. 1, 1992, pp. 39-50

Blake Nigel: "Ideal Speech Conditions, Modern Discourse and Education" *Journal of Philosophy of Education*, vol. 29, no. 3, 1995, pp. 355-67

Blake, Nigel: "The Democracy We Need: Situation, Post-Foundationalism and Enlightenment" *Journal of Philosophy of Education*, vol. 30, no. 2, 1996, pp. 215-238

Blake, Nigel: "A Postmodernism Worth Bothering About: A Rejoinder to

Cole, Hill and Rikowski" *British Journal of Educational Studies*, vol. 45, no. 3, 1997, pp. 293-305

Bookchin, Murray: *The Philosophy of Social Ecology*. Essays on Dialectical Naturalism, Jaipur: Rawat, 1996 (2nd American edition 1994)

Bryant Christopher G.A.: *Practical Sociology*. Post-empiricism and the Reconstruction of Theory and Application, Cambridge: Polity Press, 1995

Buber, Martin: *Between Man and Man*, transl. Ronald Gregor Smith, Boston: Beacon, 1961 ([1]1947)

Buber, Martin: *I and Thou*, transl. Ronald Gregor Smith, 2nd edition, New York: Charles Scribner's, 1958

The Cambridge Dictionary of Philosophy, ed. Robert Audi, Cambridge: C.U.P., 1995

Carlson, Dennis: "Making Progress: Progressive Education in the Postmodern" *Educational Theory*, vol. 45, no. 3, 1995, pp. 337-357

Carr, Wilfred: "What is an Educational Practice?" *Journal of Philosophy of Education*, vol. 21, no. 2, 1987, pp. 163-175

Carr, Wilfred: "Education and Democracy: confronting the postmodernist challenge" *Journal of Philosophy of Education*, vol. 29, no. 1, 1995, pp. 75-91

Chakrabarti, Mohit: "Re-assessing Non-violence: The Gandhian Challenge" *Gandhi Marg*, no. 105, December 1987, pp. 538-546

Chatterjee, Partha: *A Possible India*. Essays in Political Criticism, Delhi: O.U.P., 1997

Chattopadhyaya, Debiprasad: *Indian Philosophy*. A Popular Introduction, New Delhi: People's Publishing House, 1986 (1964)

Nhilde, V.G.: *Society and Knowledge*, London: Allen & Unwin, 1956

Cole, Mike/Hill, Dave: "Games of Despair and Rhetorics of Distance: postmodernism, education and reaction" *British Journal of Sociology of Education*, vol. 16, no. 2, 1995, pp. 165-182

Cole, Mike/Hill, Dave/Rikowski, Glenn: "Between Postmodernism and Nowhere: The Predicament of the Postmodernist" *British Journal of Educational Studies*, Vol. 45, no. 2, 1997, pp. 187-200

Collins, Jim: *Uncommon Cultures*. Popular Culture and Postmodernism, New York: Routledge, 1989

Dallmayr, Fred: "Modernization and Postmodernization: Wither India" *Alternatives*, Vol. 17, no. 4, 1992, pp. 421-452

Devaraja, N.K.: *The Limits of Disagreement*. An Essay on Reasoning in Humanistic Disciplines, Shimla: Indian Institute of Advanced Study, 1993

Dewey, John: *Intelligence in the Modern World*. John Dewey's Philosophy. Edited and with an Introduction by Joseph Ratner, New York: Random House, 1939

Dewey, John: *On Experience, Nature and Freedom*. Edited and with an Introduction by Richard J. Bernstein, New York: The Liberal Arts Press, 1960

Dewey, John: *On Education*. Edited and with an Introduction by Reginald D. Archambault, New York: The Modern Library, 1964

Dews, Peter: *The Limits of Disenchantment*, Essays on Contemporary European Philosophy, London: Verso, 1995

Dixon, Robert M.W.: *What is Language?* A New Approach to Linguistic Description, London: Longmans, 1966 (1965)

Dreyfus, Hubert L./Rabinow, Paul: What is Maturity? Habermas and Foucault on 'What Is Enlightenment?' in: David Couzens Hoy (ed.): *Foucault: A Critical Reader*, Oxford: Blackwell, 1989 (1986), pp. 109-121

Dworkin, Gerald: *The Theory and Practice of Autonomy*, Cambridge: C.U.P., 1989 (1988)

Edwards, Paul (ed.): *The Encyclopedia of Philosophy*, 8 vols., New York: Macmillan & The Free Press, 1967

Fanon, Frantz: *A Dying Colonialism*, transl. Haakon Chevalier, Harmondsworth: Penguin, 1970 (French original 1959)

Fanon, Frantz: *The Wretched of the Earth*, transl. Constance Farrington, Harmondsworth: Penguin, 1977 (French original 1961)

Feyerabend, Paul: *Killing Time*. The Autobiography of Paul Feyerabend, Chicago: Chicago University Press, 1995

Flew, Antony: *A Dictionary of Philosophy*, London: Macmillan, 1979

Freire, Paulo: *Pedagogy of the Oppressed*, New York: Seabury, 1970 (1968)

Freire, Paulo: *Cultural Action for Freedom*, Harmondsworth: Penguin, 1977 (1970)

Fromm, Erich: *On Disobedience and Other Essays*, London: Routledge & Kegan Paul, 1984

Fromm, Erich: *Jenseits der Illusionen*. Die Bedeutung von Marx und Freud (Beyond the Chains of Illusion. The Significance of Marx and Freud), originally published in 1962, in: Erich Fromm, Gesamtausgabe

(Collected Works), ed. Rainer Funk, vol. IX: Sozialistischer Humanismus and Humanistische Ethik (Socialistic Humanism and Humanistic Ethics), Munchen: dtv, 1989 (1981), pp. 37-157

Gress, David R.: "The Drama of Modern Western Identity" *Orbis*, vol. 41, no, 4, 1997, pp. 525-544

Gupta, Dipankar: "Can postmodernism be universalised? Derrida and Baudrillard in the tropics" *Contributions to Indian Sociology*, vol, 29, nos. 1 & 2, 1995, pp. 393-407

Habermas, Jurgen: *Toward a Rational Society*. Student Protest, Science, and Politics, transl. Jeremy J. Shapiro, London: Heinemann, 1971

Habermas, Jurgen: *Communication and the Evolution of Society*, transl. Thomas McCarthy, Boston: Beacon, 1979

Habermas, Jurgen: Toward a reconstruction of historical materialism, in: E. Knorr-Cetina/A.V. Cicourel (eds.): *Advances in Social Theory and Methodology*. Toward an integration of micro- and macro-sociologies, Boston: Routledge & Kegan Paul, 1981, pp. 259-276

Habermas, Jurgen: *Theorie des kommunikativen Handelns*, Band 2: Zur Kritik der funktionalistischen Vernunft, Frankfurt: Suhrkamp, 1997 (1981)

Habermas, Jurgen: *The Theory of Communicative Action*, vol. 1: Reason and Rationalization of Society, London: Pluto, 1984

Habermas, Jurgen: *The New Conservatism*. Cultural Criticism and the Historians' Debate, transl. Shierry Weber Nicholsen, Cambridge: Polity Press, 1989

Hacking, Ian: The Archaeology of Foucault, in: David Couzens Hoy (ed.): *Foucault: A Critical Reader*, Oxford: Blackwell, 1989 (1986), pp. 28-40

Hamlyn, D.W.: *Perception, Learning and the Self*. Essays in the Philosophy of Psychology, London: Routledge & Kegan Paul, 1983

Harpham, Geoffrey Galt: "So...What *Is* Enlightenment? An Inquisition into Modernity" *Critical Inquiry*, Vol. 20, no. 3, Spring 1994, pp. 524-556

Hentig, Hartmut von: *Die Menschen starken, die Sachen klaren* (To strengthen human beings, to clarify subjects). Ein Pladoyer fur die Wiederherstellung der Aufklarung (A plea for the reconstruction of the Enlightenment), Stuttgart: Reclam, 1985

Hiett, P.J.: "Post modernism—A Cross-Cultural Perspective" *Asian Philosophy*, vol. 5, no. 2, 1995, pp. 197-208

Hooks, Bell: *Teaching to Transgress*. Education as the Practice of Freedom, New York Routledge, 1994

Horster, Delef: Habermas, in: Bernd Lutz (ed.): *Metzler Philosophen Lexikon*, Stuttgart: Metzler, 1989, pp. 303-307

Horster, Detlef/van Reijen, Willem: *Habermas*. An Introduction, Philadelphia: Pennbridge Books, 1992 (German original 1988)

Huxley, Julian: *Essays of a Humanist*, London: Chatto & Windus, 1964

Illich, Ivan: *Deschooling Society*, Harmondsworth: Penguin, 1977 (1971)

Illich, Ivan: *Toward a History of Needs*, New York: Bantam, 1980 (1977)

James, William: *Pragmatism* and four essays from 'The Meaning of Truth', New Delhi: Eurasia, 1975 (originally published in 1907 and 1909 respectively)

Jonathan, Ruth: "What is an Educational Practice? A Reply to Wilfred Carr" *Journal of Philosophy of Education*, vol. 21, no. 2, 1987, pp. 177-180

Jonathan, Ruth: "Liberal Philosophy of Education: a paradigm under strain" *Journal of Philosophy of Education*: vol. 29, no. 1, 1995, pp. 93-107

Kant, Immanuel: *The Philosophy of Kant*. Immanuel Kant's Moral and Political Writings, ed. Carl J. Friedrich, New York: The Modern Library, 1977 (1949)

Keith, William: "De Rhetorica Fullerae" *Philosophy of Social Sciences*, vol. 25, no. 4, 1995, pp. 488-496

Kelly, A.V.: *The Curriculum*. Theory and Practice, London: Paul Chapman, [3]1989

King, Preston (ed.): *The History of Ideas*. An Introduction to Method, London: Croom Helm, 1983

Kumar, Krishna: *Social Character of Learning*, New Delhi: Sage, 1989

Kumar, Krishna: *What is Worth Teaching?* Hyderabad: Orient Longman, 1992

Kumar, Krishna : "Listening to Gandhi" *Seminar*, no. 436, December 1995, pp. 14-19

Magee, Bryan: *Men of Ideas*. Some Creators of Contemporary Philosophy, Oxford: O.U.P., 1992 (1978)

Mannheim, Karl: The Sociology of Knowledge (from *Ideology and Utopia*, 1936), in: James E. Curtis/John W. Petras (eds.): *The Sociology of Knowledge*. A Reader, London: Duckworth, 1982 (1970), pp. 109-130

Mead, George Herbert: *On Social Psychology*. Selected Papers, ed. Anselm Strauss, Chicago: The University of Chicago Press, [2]1969 ([1]1956)

Mendus, Susan: "All the King's Horses and all the King's Men: Justifying

Higher Education" *Journal of Philosophy of Education*, vol. 26, no. 2, pp. 173-182

Merchant, Carolyn (ed.): *Key Concepts in Critical Theory: Ecology*, Jaipur: Rawat, 1996 (originally published in the USA, 1994)

Mooers, Colin: "The Illusions of Postmodernism" (A review of Terry Eagleton: The Illusions of Postmodernism, 1996) *Monthly Review*, vol. 49, no. 5, 1997, pp. 58-61

Mukerjee, Hiren: *Gandhiji*. A Study, New Delhi: People's Publishing House, 1991 (1958)

Mukherji, Arundhati: "Habermas' Pragmatic Universals" *Journal of Indian Council of Philosophical Research*, vol. XIV, no. 2, 1997, pp. 31-36

Mukhopadhyay, Pradyot Kumar: *Indian Realism*. A Rigorous Descriptive Metaphysics, Calcutta: Bagchi, 1984

Needleman, Jacob: *The Indestructible Question*. Essays on Nature, Spirit and Human Paradox, Haramondsworth: Penguin, 1994 (1992)

Neill, A.S.: Summerhill Harmondsworth: Penguin, 1982 (1962)

Olssen, Mark: "Radical Constructivism and its Failings: Anti-Realism and Individualism" *British Journal of Educational Studies*, vol. 44, no. 3, 1996, pp. 275-295

Osborne, Peter (ed.): *A Critical Sense*. Interviews with Intellectuals, London: Routledge, 1996

Osterod, Oyvind: "Antinomies of Postmodernism in International Studies" *Journal of Peace Research*, vol. 22, no. 4, 1996, pp. 385-390

Pantham, Thomas: Habermas' Practical Discourse and Gandhi's *Satyagraha*, in: Bikhu Parekh/Thomas Pantham (eds.): *Political Discourse*. Explorations in Indian and Western Political Thought, New Delhi: Sage, 1987, pp. 292-310

Paulos Mar Gregorios: *Enlightenment: East and West*. Pointers in the Quest for India's Secular Identity, Delhi: B.R. Publishing Corporation, 1989

Paulos Mar Gregorios: "On Postmodernism" *Journal of Indian Council of Philosophical Research*, vol. XIV, no. 3 1997, pp. 84-89

Peters, Michael: "Education and the Postmodern Condition: revisiting Jean-Francois Lyotard" *Journal of Philosophy of Education*, vol. 29, no. 3, 1995, pp. 387-400

Peukert, Helmu: "Basic Problems of a Critical Theory of Education" *Journal of Philosophy of Education*, vol. 27, no. 2, 1993, pp. 159-170

Popkewitz, Thomas: "The production of reason and power: curriculum history and intellectual traditions" *Journal of Curriculum Studies*, vol. 29, no. 2, 1997, pp. 131-164

Pusey, Michael: Jurgen Habermas: reason and the evolution in culture, in: Diane J. Austin-Broos (ed.): *Creating Culture*. Profiles in the study of culture, Sydney: Allen & Unwin, 1987, pp. 194-209

Quicke, John: "Self, Modernity and a Direction for Curriculum Reform" *British Journal of Educational Studies*, vol. 44, no. 4, 1996, pp. 364-376

Rajan, R. Sundara: *Towards a Critique of Cultural Reason*, Delhi: O.U.P., 1987

Rorty, Richard: *Contingency, Irony, and solidarity*, Cambridge: C.U.P., 1989

Roy, M.N.: *New Humanism*. A Manifesto, Delhi: Ajanta, 1981 (1939)

Russell, Bertrand: *Human Knowledge*. Its Scope and Limits, London: Routledge, 1992 (1948)

Said, Edward: *Orientalism*, Harmondsworth: Penguin, 1995 (1978)

Santayana, George : *Scepticism and Animal Faith*. Introduction to a System of Philosophy, n.p.: Dover, 1955 (1923)

Seki-Otu, Ato: Fanon's Dialectic of Experience, Cambridge, Mass.: Harvard University Press, 1996

Sharp, Gene: Non-violence: Moral Principle or Political Technique? in: Verinder Grover (ed.): *Gandhi and Politics in India*, New Delhi: Deep & Deep, 1987, pp. 29-53

Smeyers, Paul: "Education and the Educational Project I: the atmosphere of post-modernism" *Journal of Philosophy of Education*, vol. 29, no. 1, 1995 a, pp. 109-119

Smeyers, Paul: "Education and the Educational Project II: do we still care about it?" *Journal of Philosphy of Education*, vol. 29, no. 3, 1995 b, pp. 401-413

Spinosa, Charles/Dreyfus, Hubert L.: "Two Kinds of Anti-essentialism and Their Consequences" *Critical Inquiry*, vol. 22, no. 4, Summer 1996, pp. 735-763

Standish, Paul: "Postmodernism and the Education of the Whole Person" *Journal of Philosophy of Education*, vol. 29, no. 1, 1995, pp. 121-135

St. John's College (ed.): *Catalog 1996-1997*

Tait, Katharine: *My Father Bertrand Russell*, Bristol: Thoemmes Press, 1996 (1995)

The Times Literary Supplement, November 28, 1997, p. 28

Vinoba: *Selections from Vinoba*, compiled by Vishwanath Tandon, Varanasi: Sarva Seva Sangh Prakashan, 1981

Waismann, F.: *The Principles of Linguistic Philosophy*, ed. R. Harre, London: Macmillan, 1971 (1965)

Wardekker, Willem L./Miedema, Siebren: "Critical Pedagogy: An Evaluation and Direction for Reformation" *Curriculum Inquiry*, vol. 27, no. 1, 1997, pp. 45-61 *Weber, Max: Basic Concepts in Sociology*, transl. H.P. Secher, London: Owen, 1978 (1962)

Weber, Max: *Basic Concepts in Sociology*, Transl. H.P. Secher, London: Owen, 1978 (1962)

White, S.K.: *The Recent Work of Jurgen Habermas*, Cambridge: C.U.P., 1988

Wittgenstein, Ludwig: *Philosophical Investigations*, ed. G.E.M. Anscombe and R. Rhees, transl. G.E.M. Anscombe, Oxford: Blackwell, 1973 (1953)

Wynne, John P.: *Theories of Education*, An Introduction to the Foundations of Education, New York: Harper & Row, 1963

Yutang, Lin (ed.): *The Wisdom of Confucius*, New York: The Modern Library, 1966 (1938)

Index